NEW DAD TODDLERS HACKS

Strategies and Tools for
Disciplining, Potty Training,
Sleeping Routines, and Managing
Toddler Emotions

By William Harding

Just For you!

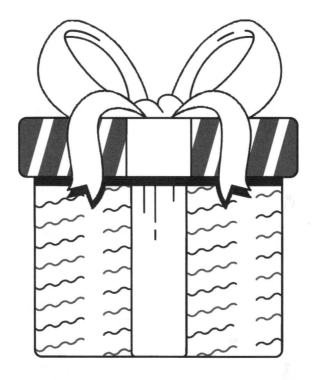

A FREE GIFT TO OUR READERS

10 Step **Action** plan that you can download now. Feel confident and prepared for your new born right now!

http://williamhardingauthor.com/

Table of Contents

Introduction vi

Chapter 1
Diving Into the Gene Pool: Nature vs. Nurture, Personality, and
Developmental Milestones 10

Chapter 2
The 3 P's of Potty Training: How To Know When Your Toddler's
Toilet Time Has Arrived 24

Chapter 3
Picky Eaters Anonymous: How to Survive Your Toddler's
Selective Tastes 34

Chapter 4
Slumber Struggles: Strategies You Can Use to Solve Sleep-related
Issues 45

Chapter 5
Find Shelter! The Terrible Two Tornado is Here 56

Chapter 6
Dealing with Discipline: Techniques to Teach Your Toddler
Consequences with Compassion 66

Chapter 7
Cultivating Character and Building Better Humans 77

Chapter 8
Meeting Near the Tiny Water Cooler: Why Socializing Your
Toddler is Essential 87

Chapter 9
Clothing Chaos and Wardrobe Wars: Dressing Your Toddler for
Success 97

Chapter 10
Me T.I.M.E.: The Best Way For Dads to Practice Self-Care 107

Chapter 11

Every Pilot Needs a Co-Pilot: How to Parent with a Partner....117

Conclusion..**127**

Reviews...**135**

Join the Dads Club Community...**136**

References **137**

Introduction

Picture this: your 6 AM alarm blares, a sound you've come to dread, and you stumble into the kitchen to make a cup of coffee. As your feet hit the linoleum floor and you start mentally planning out your morning, you notice a strange trail of brown and red slime leading up to your fridge. Your eyebrows furrow as you bend down, swiping your finger across the sticky residue and smelling the scent of peanuts.

"Well, at least it's only peanut butter," you sigh, wiping your hand on a paper towel. You walk forward, half awake, and wonder how your child even got a hold of the peanut butter. Opening the door to your fridge, you see your little chef has made a peanut butter and jelly sandwich using your favorite tie as bread. You rub your temples, look at the baby fence you forgot to close, and start cleaning up. So begins another day in Dadland.

While this may sound ridiculous to a non-parent, this situation is an average morning for the father of an unruly child. Chances are, you're feeling like a deer caught in the headlights of parenting right now. The adorable coos and toothless smiles of infancy are gone, and the turmoil of toddlerhood has arrived at your door. You've likely found yourself wrestling with a barrage of dilemmas lately, and you might be wondering whether to laugh, cry, or just give in and start eating your kid's hand-crafted peanut butter and silk sandwich.

Juggling your work, relationship, and fatherly responsibilities can leave even the strongest man teetering on the edge of sanity. But believe me, you aren't alone. I, and millions of dads just like me, have made it through this stage of fatherhood. It's perfectly normal to feel frustrated, flustered, and even terrified. Many fathers have found themselves knee-deep in the chaos of toddlerhood, pulling out their hair and second-guessing their parenting skills.

But hey, that's why you're here! Everyone could use a helping hand occasionally, and with this book, I hope to share a few of the tips I've learned throughout my fatherhood journey. As an avid writer and long-time nerd, I've always felt the need to research and take notes about my experiences; my time as a parent has been no different. What I've assembled here is a handbook for toddler dad survival, complete with all the practical strategies you need to navigate real-life parenting challenges. In addition, I've included a series of "hacks" with each chapter that you can use to make your life easier.

Some of the skills I'll share include:

- How to Determine Disposition from Your Toddler's Genetics

- The 3 P's of Potty Training

- How to Deal With a Picky Eater

- Solutions to Help Get Your Toddler to Sleep

- The Best Ways to Traverse the Terrible Twos

- Positive and Empathetic Discipline Tactics

- Techniques for Instilling Valuable Personality Traits

- Strategies for Socialization

- Quick and Convenient Capsule Wardrobes

- How to Avoid Burnout and Find Time for Self-Care

- The Best Methods for Collaborating with a Co-parent

The information in this book is the result of years of triumphs, failures, laughter, and tears. Everything written here that doesn't come from my research is taken from my experiences as a dad to three beautiful, sometimes terribly mischievous, kids. It's the wisdom I wish I had when I was a new dad, staring wide-eyed at my first child, pondering, "Now what?" I've made the mistakes you are terrified of making and come out the other side stronger and wiser. Now, I wish to share that wisdom with you.

Before I had the insights I'm about to share, the toddler years were a labyrinth of uncertainty and confusion. But once I found these proven strategies and techniques, the fog of uncertainty lifted and things became surprisingly manageable. While you may be stressed out right now, struggling with particular challenges, or arguing with your co-parent, I'm confident the information within these pages can change that.

After reading this book, you will be able to navigate the tumultuous toddler years with newfound confidence. Picture yourself effortlessly balancing work, fun, and fatherhood, brimming with newfound parenting prowess. Imagine co-parenting in harmony with your partner, leaving conflict and tension in the dust. That's the life waiting for you at the end of this book.

Let these pages be your companion as you traverse the ups and downs of fatherhood. This guide can offer support, advice, and (I hope) a hearty laugh when you need it most. Together, we'll make sure that you don't just survive; you thrive! So buckle up, brace yourself, and get ready for a wild ride. It's time to navigate the thrilling adventure that is raising a toddler.

Let's get started!

Chapter 1

Diving Into the Gene Pool: Nature vs. Nurture, Personality, and Developmental Milestones

Before our first child was born, my wife and I constantly talked about who our daughter would take after more. Would she have my wife's stunning eyes and long flowing hair? Would she inherit my height and tower over the other children? Most importantly, would she be able to dunk? We also considered the possibility our daughter would be nothing like us (which would be perfectly okay!) but secretly hoped, like many parents, she would get a mix of the best traits we both had to offer.

After our daughter arrived, we were utterly amazed by how much she seemed to resemble both of us, right down to her little quirks. Her smile was identical to my wife's, capable of lighting up the room on the gloomiest of days. Our daughter would also furrow her brow whenever she became frustrated, something I've done since I was young. As she continued to grow, I noticed that the similarities didn't stop there, and I became curious. How much did genetics and her environment influence her personality and development? To answer this question, we'll start by looking at the role that genetics can play in shaping your child.

What Role Do Genes Play?

Genes aren't just responsible for the color of your toddler's eyes or how tall they'll grow; they have a much more significant impact on their growth, behavior, and development. From how they think to how they socialize, genetics can majorly influence what type of person your toddler will grow up to be.

Here are some of the roles that genetics play in toddler development:

- **The Way Their Brains Are Wired:** Genetic factors can influence the brain in many ways, impacting learning processes, memory, attention span, and even emotional regulation. Genes could be the reason your little angel becomes a little tyrant when they're hungry, why they become a social butterfly during playtime, and why they may get easily frustrated at times.

- **How They Influence and Interact with Others:** Genes can also determine how our children influence others. For example, a happy, smiling baby may get more social interaction and positive reinforcement than one who is prone to crying fits. On the other hand, a child who is a bit more shy may struggle to be sociable. Another example would be a child with low self-control; because of this genetic trait, they are more likely to experience frustration from caregivers or punishments for breaking rules.

- **How They Respond to Their Environment:** Our little ones' genes can also define how they respond to their environments, which can significantly impact the rate at which they hit certain developmental milestones. One child may go into hysterics the second a dog begins to bark, while another may run over because they associate a puppy with playtime. Take note of how your child interacts with different stimuli, particularly in stressful situations. This can allow you to create an environment that caters to their specific needs or address behavioral issues that may hinder them later in life.

- **Their Level of Curiosity and Interest:** Genes can influence how much our children seek out new experiences and what activities they prefer. You may discover your child is dazzled by the visual brilliance of a fireworks show but isn't able to sit still for story time. Your toddler may also frequently run off to find the nearest piece of furniture to climb, while another child may be content sitting and drawing for hours on end. Look at how your children explore and what activities they prefer, and encourage them to learn more about the things they love to do.

Despite the importance of genetics in child development, they're not the end-all and be-all. While your toddler may have inherited certain traits and tendencies, it's important to remember that you can help shape their behavior by working with their natural characteristics and disposition. The best way to do this is by understanding the variety of temperaments and personality traits your child may have.

Types of Temperament and Personality Traits

Every toddler is made up of a unique combination of movements, sleep patterns, moods, and sensitivities. Your child's temperament will be defined by a number of factors; in many cases, these factors determine how they behave in different situations. By understanding these traits and how they apply to your little one, you'll be able to adjust your parenting style to ensure you're supporting their growth to the best of your ability.

- **Level of Activity:** How much is your tiny tyke on the move? Do they seem to bounce off the walls, or are they perfectly happy sitting and watching a movie? Finding out whether your child has a high activity level or low activity level can help you determine what activities to plan, decide what toys to purchase, and even show you what types of careers they may want to pursue later in life.

- **Biological Rhythms:** Eating, sleeping, and, yes, even pooping. Your child will settle into various patterns that will (hopefully) make it easier to predict their natural needs. This may take some time, and it's important not to fret. Your toddler may go through phases where their sleep is more erratic, they want to eat at strange times, or they go through diapers at a frightening pace. Understanding their rhythms and guiding them toward healthier patterns can not only help them develop, but help you retain your sanity.

- **Approachability and Tendency to Withdraw:** Does your child tend to approach new situations or people with excitement, or do they withdraw at the sight of potentially stressful stimuli? Some toddlers will run headlong into the unknown (which can be both beneficial and harmful), while others may show caution when presented with something or someone new. Finding out the level of approachability your child displays can assist you in keeping them safe. On the other hand, if they seem a bit too reserved, it can help you guide them out of their shell to interact more with the world around them.

- **Mood:** While toddlers are unlikely to have full control of their emotions, your child will nevertheless have a tendency to display specific mood patterns. Your toddler may constantly be a little ball of sunshine, smiling happily as they drop food from their high chair as you wearily make your morning coffee. On the other hand, your kid could be a bit more cranky, prone to crying, or quick to anger. Neither disposition is the "right" one; most likely, your child will go through phases where they exhibit one or both frequently.

- **Reactivity, Sensitivity, and Distractibility:** How does your child interact with various environments? Do they have strong reactions or jump right to large emotional displays? Do they tend to be sensitive to certain sounds, smells, and foods? Are they able to focus, even in a chaotic space? Figuring out how your child reacts to different situations, what stimuli they are most sensitive to, and what their attention span is like are all essential components of designing your unique parenting strategy.

- **Persistence and Adaptability:** These traits are all about how your child reacts when presented with a challenge or new situation. You may find they tend to persist even when a task is tricky. This is usually a good thing; unless that task happens to be spreading peanut butter along every inch of your brand-new kitchen counters (a project my daughter delightfully took on). You may also find that your child can adapt to situations if a solution isn't obvious. Again, this is great in theory. It isn't so great if they adapt to you hiding the peanut butter on the top shelf by continuing their painting project with every other liquid they can find. Learning how persistent and adaptable your child is is great for deciding what challenges to present them with. It can also, unfortunately, force you to learn how to clean peanut butter out of those hard-to-reach places under the oven.

It's important to remember that all of these traits exist on a spectrum, and your child will likely not fit neatly into any particular category. Again, genetics may set the baseline for some of these, but overall, their environment will play a big part in shaping their behavior as they grow. While genetics may be important, it's also our job as parents to understand our children and create environments that work with their personality traits, not against them.

Crafting an Environment That Fits Your Toddler

Using what you've learned about your child's genetic pre-dispositions and traits, you can create an environment that perfectly fits their needs and natural tendencies. Now, the way you do this is entirely up to you, but the environment you build should be based on love, care, and positive reinforcement. This will help keep your toddler's self-esteem high and give them the emotional security they'll need to comfortably explore. You'll also want to model good behavior in your own actions and environment, as children often mimic their parents. Staying patient and positive in your interactions (even those that aren't directly with your child) can encourage them to have a similar attitude.

Here are a couple of tips you can use to ensure the physical and emotional environment you create is optimally designed to encourage growth and development.

Tip #1: *Create "Zones" Inside and Outside Your Home*

One way to set the foundation for a good physical environment is by establishing various "zones" for your child to grow within. These zones can be designed in any way you choose, and should be created with your child's unique personality in mind. One example would be the "Yes Zone," a place where your child can explore to their heart's content without any risk of hazard. This zone can have educational toys, books, and spaces where they can move about and learn to interact with various objects. A "Yes Zone" can help your child develop cognitively, as well as allow them to express themselves creatively. It's important that this area is fully toddler-proofed: that means no sharp corners, no heights they could climb to and fall from, and no dangerous implements they can get their hands on.

This area will be perfect for increasing your child's independence, as you'll be able to let them explore it without the need for constant supervision. This can also increase their ability to regulate their own emotions. Your child will have to learn how to manage their feelings and impulses without constantly having to seek out your support, which is an invaluable skill to learn as they grow. That being said, it's probably still a good idea to have a baby cam or monitor with you so you can check up on them frequently.

Another zone example, which will likely be outside, is the "physical" zone. This should have everything they need to climb, play, and run about. Staying active is important for people of all ages; for your toddler, play is a great way to help them develop their gross motor skills. Not only that but letting your toddler burn off their boundless energy can make bedtime a lot easier to deal with. You can join them in their adventures as well, dancing or running with them to strengthen your bond.

Tip #2: *Establish Routines, But Don't Hinder Independence*

Part of the environment you create for your child will hinge on a careful balance of planned routine and the freedom to let them choose some aspects of their own lives. It's important to set boundaries and create a routine for your child to follow. This teaches them that there are certain rules they will need to adhere to as they grow and helps them understand the consequences that come when those rules are broken. Routines can also be comforting to children and add an element of predictability to their lives (and yours.)

Regular meal times, bedtimes, and play times will help set your toddler into a familiar rhythm that will make day-to-day life far smoother.

While routines and boundaries are essential, you'll want to make sure they aren't too rigid. Your toddler will eventually grow up into an adult who will have their own sense of identity and make their own decisions. You can set up the building blocks of this future independence by letting them choose certain elements of their environment. If snack time is coming up, let them choose between two different snacks. If bedtime usually comes with a story, let them select from a few different titles. Give your child positive reinforcement when they make a choice, as this will encourage them to engage in more decision-making in the future. Not only that, but choice can also make an activity your child generally dislikes a bit easier. If your child hates baths, but you let them choose the bath toys, you'll be surprised how quickly their attitude changes!

Tip #3: *Don't Forget About Playdates*

Socialization is crucial for toddlers, and you'll want to set up playdates or join groups that let groups of children play together safely. These events can help reinforce many of the lessons your child has learned, as well as expand their ability to communicate and problem-solve. You'll be able to see whether your child is able to follow the rules established around play time (no hitting, sharing toys, etc.) and monitor their emotional responses to different stimuli. Again, this is where a knowledge of their personality traits and disposition comes in handy. If your child is shy, you may take this time to encourage them to get out of their shell a bit. If your toddler is having trouble sharing, you can use playdates as a way to break them of this bad habit.

What activities a playdate or playgroup involves can vary. It's good to have a creative activity like finger painting available, as well as a physical activity that they can safely do in the provided area. This time can also serve as an opportunity for you to converse with other parents. Talk about the various challenges or strategies you have been using in your parenting, discuss tips you may have for each other on dealing with toddler-specific issues, and even share certain materials like hand-me-down clothes or old toys. You can also take a break from the baby talk, as too much can be overwhelming. Talk about what TV shows you've been watching, sports teams you've been following, or upcoming trips you have planned with your spouse. Remember, your toddler isn't the only one who needs to socialize!

Toddler Developmental Milestones

While genes and environment will both have an important role in your toddler's development, remember that every child is unique. Your child may not have the exact same developmental milestones as another, or they may reach them at a different pace. So even though these are mile*stones,* they aren't set in stone; they function more as a guide.

That being said, I've provided a general framework below for the types of milestones and timeframes that you may see during your child's development. This framework is separated into four different categories: physical development, language development, cognitive development, and social/emotional development.

Physical Development Milestones

When it comes to physical milestones, your little one is bound to surprise you with their newfound skills. Soon, the days where you can be 100% certain your child is exactly where you left them will be gone (hooray?) From wobbly first steps to scaling furniture like a tiny Spider-Man, here's what to expect:

- **12 months:** Walking (with assistance), holding on to furniture, picking up bits of food with their thumb and pointer finger

- **12-18 months:** Taking a few steps on their own, holding crayons, drawing and scribbling, building block towers

- **18-24 months:** walking for longer periods of time unassisted, climbing onto chairs without help, attempting to use a spoon

- **24-36 months:** Running, climbing onto furniture or equipment on the playground, alternating feet while climbing stairs, jumping with both feet, standing on toes, kicking toy balls, attempting to use a fork, showing interest in using the toilet and potty training

You can assist your toddler in reaching these milestones by letting them safely engage in physical activities. Join them in running, dancing, painting, and playing, whether that be indoors or outdoors. Make sure to keep any play spaces free from dangerous objects, and watch them closely (especially during the earlier stages.)

Language Development Milestones

Language milestones relate to your child's growing ability to understand and express themselves, whether that be through verbal communication (words, gestures, etc.) or non-verbal communication. You'll slowly learn your child's communication style over these stages, which can help you further support their language development.

- **12 months:** Repeating and mimicking the words or sounds they hear (so be careful what you say!)

- **12-18 months:** Saying single words like "mama" and "dada," communicating via gestures like waving and nodding their head

- **18-24 months:** Understanding and following simple instructions, pointing to objects or pictures when asked

- **24-36 months:** Using simple phrases to communicate and answer simple questions. Some examples include "More food, please" or answering questions like "What is your name?" Toddlers may also begin to engage in short conversations during this time.

There are a number of ways to encourage this type of development, including talking to your toddler often, reading books allowed to them, and including them in conversations with other children and adults.

Cognitive Development Milestones

Your child's cognitive development will define their ability to solve problems, learn new subjects, and understand the world around them. This will also be the stage where they begin to understand the idea of short-term planning (which, for my daughter, involved leaving her legos out in just the right way, so I always managed to step on them.)

Here are some of the cognitive milestones you can expect.

- **12 months:** Exploring and beginning to understand cause-and-effect relationships. An example of this would be the response electronic toys have to touch (i.e., they press a button, and music begins to play)

- **12-18 months:** Recognizing the look, feel, and name of familiar objects, identifying familiar people, and engaging in simple problem-solving (like getting a cookie out of a cookie jar)

- **18-24 months:** Mimicking certain behaviors (like copying the movements you engage in when sweeping or doing other chores), playing with toys in simple ways

- **24-36 months:** Showing a higher interest in stories, engaging in more complex play (alone or with other children), developing an understanding of other's emotions, and beginning to understand the concept of time

It's important to provide as many opportunities for your child to explore and engage with their environment as possible, as well as give them the right puzzles, toys, and art supplies they need to expand their creativity and problem-solving abilities.

Social and Emotional Development Milestones

Your child's ability to express and regulate their emotions, as well as how they form relationships, will grow rapidly during this time period. Some developmental milestones for this category include:

- **12 months:** Showing affection for their parents and other familiar people, playing simple games like patty cake

- **12-18 months:** Learning to cope with the distress of separation from parents or caregivers, starting to engage in parallel play (playing without influencing others) while socializing with other children

- **18-24 months:** Developing empathy and appropriate responses to others, establishing preferences for certain activities and toys, or playing with multiple toys at once

- **24-36 months:** Expanding their sense of independence and autonomy, engaging in cooperative play with other children, learning to express emotions through verbal (like simple phrases), developing friendships with other children

One of the big ways to help them develop in this category is to model the behavior you wish them to exhibit. Stay patient when your child has crying fits or outbursts, and try to help them understand their feelings. This can go a long way toward empathy development and emotional self-regulation.

From Pool to Potty: Let's Talk Toilets

One important milestone that many parents eagerly await is the transition from diapers to potty training. Now that we understand a bit more about genetics, environments, and development milestones, let's talk about something every parent looks forward to: No more diapers! In our next chapter, we'll discuss the best ways to recognize that your child is ready for bathroom training, the 3 P's of potty training, and some common misconceptions you may have about the process.

Dad Hacks from Chapter 1

Development Hack #1: Embrace Your One-of-a-kind Child. Your toddler isn't going to be the exact same as any other child on the planet, and that's a good thing! Learning your child's unique strengths and weaknesses will help you support them as they continue to develop.

Development Hack #2: Don't Be Afraid to Change Your Style. You may find that your child (whether due to genetics or environment) isn't responding to certain elements of your parenting style. Never be afraid to switch it up!

Development Hack #3: Create the Most Nurturing Environment Possible. While boundaries and discipline are important, don't forget to prioritize praise, positivity, and encouragement. The more nurturing an environment is, the more comfortable your child will be in moving through development milestones.

Development Hack #4: Give Them the Space to Be Independent. Make sure to let your child make some simple decisions and tackle certain tasks with limited supervision. Independence will only get more important as they age, and creating the building blocks now can make this process easier later on.

Development Hack #5: Patience is Key. Your child may struggle to reach certain developmental milestones, and that is perfectly okay. You may also have difficulties finding a parenting style that works, and that's okay too. Be patient with them and yourself, and remember that parenting is an ever-evolving journey.

Chapter 2

The 3 P's of Potty Training: How to Know When Your Toddler's Toilet Time Has Arrived

While it may seem insignificant to someone without children, any parent knows the importance of the "potty training" milestone. With each of our three children, my wife and I looked forward to the day we would no longer have to carry the diaper bag on trips or search frantically for a changing table. But, of course, potty training in and of itself can be its own chore, and it's normal for children to struggle to overcome this obstacle.

In fact, according to *The No Cry Training Solution: Gentle Ways to Help Your Child Say Goodbye to Diapers* by Elizabeth Pantley, **80% of children** experience setbacks during the toilet training process. I can tell you from experience that this statistic can be higher; our children each had their own unique difficulties during toilet training. Some of the issues they faced may have come from the fact that, in some cases, they weren't quite ready to give up diapers. Because of this, it's essential to look for the signs that your child is prepared to transition into the realm of the restroom.

4 Signs That Your Toddler Is Ready for Potty Training

Sign #1: *Barging in on Bathroom Time*

Curiosity about the bathroom is one of the first signs you'll see that your toddler may be ready for toilet training. You may notice them searching around, asking to sit on the toilet, or simply opening the bathroom door anytime you forget to lock it. While having a bathroom bandit break-in can be frustrating, make sure to encourage this curiosity (while setting appropriate boundaries). Explain to them how the toilet works, how to use toilet paper, and get them comfortable with the idea of using the bathroom themselves.

Sign #2: *They Begin to Outgrow Diapers*

Another sign you'll notice is that your toddler is starting to outgrow their diapers, both physically and mentally. They may begin to get annoyed with the feeling of a dirty diaper, possibly trying to remove them on their own. This can involve them asking how to pull their pants up and down, another important step in potty training readiness. In addition, you may notice that their diapers are staying dry for far longer than usual. A good rule of thumb is any amount of time over 2 hours; this means that your toddler is developing control of their bladder and bowels (or they were in the middle of a Peppa Pig binge and didn't want to get up.) Dry diapers can indicate they may be ready to hop on the porcelain throne. Make sure to give them positive reinforcement during all of these steps, as this can make their transition into training that much easier.

Sign #3: *More Bathroom Time Communication*

You may find your toddler is beginning to communicate their bathroom needs more often, letting you and your partner know they need to "go" with a combination of words, facial expressions, or gestures. This shows they are starting to understand the feelings associated with bathroom time and that they may be ready for introductory lessons. These lessons can involve giving them simple instructions, like "Show me how to get to the bathroom" or "Let's sit on the potty." (or if you are dealing with my kids, "Please stop talking about poop at the dinner table, we have guests over.") Jokes aside, these open and honest conversations will set the foundation for more in-depth toilet training later on.

Sign #4: *They Seem Physically Ready and Interested in Toilet Training*

Toddlers need to reach a certain level of physical development before they can safely and efficiently use the toilet. You want to ensure that your child can sit and walk without assistance before you consider beginning the potty training process. It's also important they have a certain level of coordination and control over their fine motor skills, as they'll need to be able to take off their clothing, balance while sitting, use toilet paper, and operate the toilet handle. In addition, you want to make sure they are ready mentally. One sign we ran into with our youngest son was him telling us he "wanted to be a big boy" and use the potty. This is surprisingly common, with many children wanting to emulate the behaviors of their parents and others around them. They see you using the bathroom, so they want to as well!

The 3 P's: Preparation, Practice, and Positive Reinforcement

Once you've determined your child is ready, it's time to start the potty training process. This can be broken down into three distinct categories: **preparation**, **practice**, and **positive reinforcement**. Now, this isn't a set-in-stone set of instructions, as your child may not linearly progress through this milestone. So don't let them get frustrated if they face difficulties with one aspect. Instead, move on to a different topic, and circle back once they've had some time to absorb the information. For now, let's start with the first P: Preparation.

Preparation: Talkin' Toilet With Your Toddler

To start the preparation process, you'll want to open a dialogue about the potty with your toddler and get them their own mini-throne. Purchase a child-training potty chair and put it in your bathroom, then give your child time to get comfortable with it. You can even have them pick out one online or in a store; this will generate even more interest in the training process. The goal is to get them accustomed to the idea that this potty is what they should associate with bathroom time.

You'll also want to have a frank discussion about bodily functions. Yes, that means it's time to introduce them to the words like "pee" and "poop," which I guarantee they will say nonstop anytime you are waiting in line at a coffee shop. Explain (in simple terms) what happens to food after eating it, how the waste elimination process works, and make sure to mention that everybody (including Daddy and Mommy) poops!

Speaking of Everybody Poops, reading books about toilet training is an excellent way to help your toddler better understand how toilet time will work from now on. You can combine this commode curriculum with demonstrations, like dumping a dirty diaper in the toilet or (and I know this may sound a bit weird) bringing them into the bathroom while you use the restroom. All of this will facilitate their future time in the facilities and make the implementation of toilet training techniques far easier.

Practice: Almost Time to Ditch Those Diapers!

Now that your toddler is privy to the privy, it's time to put some of that information into action. You can start by plopping your tot down onto the toilet fully clothed, as this can ease them into the idea of using the potty. While they are seated, let them ask questions and try to discern how much they know about toilet time. Depending on what type of potty you choose, it may have all of the same features as a regular toilet, including a handle to flush. While they may not use that quite yet, it's good to ask them whether they understand how different parts of the toilet work for later on.

Another activity they'll need to practice is no longer wearing diapers. While they may be getting tired of them, diapers have been a major part of your toddler's life for a long time. There can be an adjustment period during the switch to underwear that can lead to frustration and crying fits. Don't fret! This is temporary and can be mitigated in various ways. One way that worked for us was to let our children pick out their own underwear. Superheroes, puppies, flowers, whatever pattern made them more interested in making the switch.

Setting a schedule for potty time can also be helpful, even if your toddler doesn't have to go. Encourage them to sit on the seat after meals or before they go to bed; staying consistent with this routine can help them adjust to the independent element of going to the bathroom. The "before bed" potty time is especially important. I had one particular night when I was washing sheets at 3 am, only hours before a big day at work. When I made the mistake of telling my wife, I got to hear the cute nickname "Poop Sheets" for weeks after. So don't be like me; make sure your children go for a nighttime potty!

Positive Reinforcement: Hugs and High Fives Are Key

As with any journey, it's important to keep your little one's spirits up and let them know you are proud of them. As I mentioned before, there will almost certainly be setbacks and accidents along the way. It's important not to scold or get angry; your toddler is trying their best, and potty training isn't easy. When accidents do happen, make sure to keep the tone light with responses like "It's okay, bud, we'll get it next time!" and "This happens to everyone; no need to worry." Positivity can go a long way to keeping your child on the toilet training track.

Speaking of track, you can track their progress and celebrate when they reach certain milestones. Create a colorful chart and let them choose stickers they can apply to it every time they use the toilet. Have a celebratory dance party whenever one of these stickers goes on, and make sure your toddler understands how important their achievement is. Of course, you don't want to go overboard with these celebrations, as your child may lose some enthusiasm or feel pressured to succeed. But setting goals and reaching them isn't only a valuable skill for potty training; it's a skill they will be able to use in almost every part of their lives.

Myths Around Potty Training

As you've likely learned, with many parts of parenting, there is a lot of misinformation floating around about potty training. Some of these myths have existed for ages, while others have been created more recently by the internet and social media. Here are a few common misconceptions we can dispel about the toilet training process:

Myth: *You Have to Begin Toilet Training By a Certain Age*

If you feel like there is pressure to get toilet training started by some arbitrary age, don't worry. Children develop at different rates, and forcing your child to start training too early may cause more setbacks later on. Instead of creating arbitrary deadlines, focus on making sure your child is ready to make this transition. It may be difficult to remember this when you are changing your thousandth dirty diaper but believe me, rushing things isn't going to help.

Myth: *You Can Get Potty Training Done in a Few Days*

Just like starting early, rushing potty training will only lead to complications. The process may test your patience a bit and can take anywhere from a few weeks to a few months. Like a lot of your parenting journey, this task won't be without its challenges. Take it slow and make sure your toddler is comfortable. Once you get past the finish line, you'll be able to appreciate the accomplishment that much more, trust me!

Myth: *Punishing Your Child Can Make Them Learn More Quickly*

Remember, patience is key here. Yes, there will likely be stressful moments during potty training that may frustrate you. But yelling at your toddler or punishing them might be the worst thing you could do. For one, it may scare them away from moving past the many hurdles of the training process. It may also cause them to develop anxiety about going to the bathroom, which could mean you'll be changing diapers for months or years to come. Stay positive, give encouragement, and focus on the good rather than the bad; it will all work out in the end.

What Not To Do During Potty Training

One mistake I made early on was getting rid of diapers a bit too early, which led to some mishaps throughout the day and occasionally at night. Even while potty training, it can be helpful to wait to throw those diapers away, as they can act like training wheels during the earlier stages. Your child may even want to get rid of them right away, but it's better to be cautious. Otherwise, you may find yourself cleaning tiny pairs of pants several times a day.

You also don't want to compare your child's progress with the progress of your friend's children or other parents in any groups you may be in. Remember, every child is different, and struggling with potty training has no bearing on your ability as a parent. Just like your child will face setbacks and need encouragement, so will you. Talk with your partner if you feel like you are struggling with this stage of development, and reach out to experienced parents in your social circle. There is no one-size-fits-all approach to potty training, and you may get some advice that could help you break through a difficult obstacle.

You'll also want to leave some wiggle room in your approach and make sure to cover other potty-related basics. Hygiene is important, and you'll want to teach your toddler how to flush and wash their hands after going to the bathroom. This is another opportunity to let them pick out something and encourage further participation in their training. Let them select a fun and safe kid's soap, particularly one with a scent they'll like. My children particularly like foaming soap, and I've never had trouble getting them to wash their hands. On the other hand, I've also seen them empty an entire bottle into the toilet and create a giant foaming mess, but it's all about the victories, not the setbacks.

From Potty Training Triumphs to The Challenge: Picky Eaters

It will take a lot of effort and patience, but in the end, potty training is an incredibly rewarding process. It's not only a huge step forward for your child but a big accomplishment for any parent to achieve. Once you get there, make sure to take the time to celebrate; you deserve it!

As we move out of the bathroom and into the kitchen, let's tackle the issue of picky eaters. I've had no shortage of stress surrounding mealtimes in my time as a dad, and learning how to navigate the complicated world of toddler nutrition isn't easy. Get ready to use a bit more of that patience, and be prepared for a few flung bowls of cereal to sail your way. In our next chapter, we cover what it means to be a picky eater, a few strategies to overcome this challenge, how new foods can assist you, and a few pitfalls to avoid.

Dad Hacks from Chapter 2

Potty Training Hack #1: Make Sure Not to Rush. Every child is different, and your toddler may need more time before they are ready to try the potty. It's possible they may start the process and become overwhelmed; in those cases, it's okay to take a step back and use diapers for a bit longer. They will get there eventually!

Potty Training Hack #2: Be Open and Honest. Bodily functions can be an awkward subject for some to broach, but the more you communicate with your child, the more comfortable they will be. Answer any questions they have, and ensure they understand every step of the potty training process.

Potty Training Hack #3: Encourage Them. Encouragement and positivity go a long way, and celebrating those little victories can make all the difference. Give your child a compliment or a high-five when they successfully use the potty, and comfort them if they face a setback.

Potty Training Hack #4: Don't Forget to Have Fun. Like any subject you teach to your child, potty training should be as fun and engaging as possible. Letting your child pick out their potty and underwear, as well as providing rewards when they succeed, can all help your child be more engaged in the training process.

Potty Training Hack #5: Stay Regular (or, in This Case, Consistent). Establishing a regular bathroom schedule will get your toddler into a comfortable rhythm when it comes to potty time. It will also help cut back on the number of accidents you may face during this transitory period.

Chapter 3

Picky Eaters Anonymous: How to Survive Your Toddler's Selective Tastes

As a parent, nothing can cause your stress levels to shoot through the roof like having your child refuse to eat dinner. We have an innate need to provide for our children and make sure they don't go hungry, so when you spend an hour prepping a delicious dinner only to see it splash to the floor, it's understandable to be frustrated. Unfortunately, this picky behavior can pop up at any time and with any food. Let me tell you of the epic struggle I had with my son concerning every toddler's favorite food: broccoli.

Surprisingly enough, when I first introduced my son to this small tree-like vegetable, he didn't mind it at all. Like a lumberjack mowing down a forest with his teeth, he'd buzz through broccoli with no problem. Then one day, out of nowhere, he decided he absolutely hated it. This was devastating because, at the time, broccoli was one of the few vegetables I could consistently get him to eat. I tried to find the cause of his sudden dislike, coming to the conclusion that maybe he had noticed *I* never ate broccoli (more of a Brussels sprouts man myself) and was mimicking my behavior. So I started eating broccoli more, hoping that would entice him to get his daily greens. But alas, my son didn't take the bait, and the broccoli war continued.

So I did what I always do when I face an obstacle as a parent: research. While I wasn't far off the mark with my hunch concerning my own eating habits, it turns out there are a wide variety of reasons that a child can suddenly turn their nose up at a previously preferred snack.

Why Does Picky Eating Exist?

The cause of picky eating usually can't be narrowed down to one single factor. Instead, there can be a number of genetic, developmental, and environmental influences causing your toddler to toss their plate across the room. These factors can include:

- **Oh Look, it's Genes Again!:** Part of the issue lies in a subject we discussed heavily in Chapter 1, your toddler's genes. Turns out I was right, and my own disdain for broccoli may have been transferred to my toddler through genetics. While it took a bit of time, that genetic predisposition to dislike tiny green trees eventually showed up, causing me to scramble to find another vegetable to put on his plate.

- **Developing Taste Buds:** Like the many other forms of development your toddler is undergoing at this age, their taste buds will rapidly grow and change. Foods that were cleared to land only a few weeks ago could quickly get thrown on the "no-fly" list, and you may find yourself frantically searching the aisles for a replacement.

- **Sensory Overload:** Childhood can be a period of heightened sensitivity, and your toddler's sense of taste and smell will still be adjusting to various stimuli. It's possible that the texture of certain foods just doesn't feel right in their mouth, or the scent of some meals is unpleasant to their noses. It can be helpful to play around with different spices and meal selections to see if there are specific categories of food your child doesn't like.

- **Mealtime Rebellion:** While independence is an important value to instill in your children, that independent spirit can sometimes get in the way of proper nutrition. It's important not to fight against these streaks of culinary rebellion; instead, work with your child to help them feel more in control. Offer them a few healthy choices before you go to the store, and let them pick out the occasional treat they can have if they consistently eat their veggies.

- **Snack Shortcut:** One thing I've been guilty of during past hunger strikes is just falling back on whatever reliable foods my children will usually eat. This is easy to do if you are stressed out or behind on your sleep, and I have personally served chicken strips and ranch for three nights in a row before. Unfortunately, this sets a precedent, and your toddler may avoid eating other foods if they know eventually, you will break. Try to resist this urge, and keep their diet healthy and varied.

- **Monkey See, Monkey Do:** As we've discussed before, there is nothing your toddler will love to do more than imitate the behavior of others. This can become problematic at dinner time; if they see you chomping on a cheeseburger while they have a plate of greens, they may decide they want to eat the more "grown-up" meal. Try to eat the same foods as your toddler, at least during meals you are both having together.

- **One Bad Apple Spoils the Bunch:** Say your child eats a particularly bad carrot one day and spits it out in disgust. More than likely, the next time you give them carrots, they will shake their head and say "no!". Toddlers can form a negative association with foods due to negative or stressful encounters. Try to keep mealtime as fun and positive as possible. You'll also want to make sure that any healthy foods you are giving them, especially for the first time, are as well-prepared as possible.

- **Lack of Variation:** Having the same meal every day can get old, even for adults. Your toddler is no different, and a monotonous meal plan will likely cause them to grow tired of certain foods. Shake up the menu occasionally, slowly adding other foods so your toddler doesn't become overwhelmed. Eventually, you'll be able to build up a varied list of the foods you know they will love (that way, the next time you are having trouble, you have more options to fall back on.)

- **Not a Picky Eater, a Sicky Eater:** Sometimes your child isn't turning down a meal to be difficult; they just aren't feeling well. If your toddler refuses to eat one of their favorite meals, it may be a good time to check their temperature or see if they have any other noticeable symptoms. If they are sick, now would be a good time for comfort foods and plenty of fluids!

5 Tips to Help a "Chewsy" Child Chow Down

So what should you do if your child is acting like a miniature Gordon Ramsey, stalking around the kitchen and yelling about how "your cooking is raw"? Well, there are many tools in your cuisine cache that you use to combat a case of picky eating. Here are some tips you can use when your toddler is putting their tiny foot down and simply won't eat.

Tip #1: *Give Tiny Bites to Your Tiny Tots*

One habit that's easy to fall into when your toddler won't eat is piling their plate up high with large portions. This is part of that inherent need to provide for your child, and if they didn't eat at their last meal, you'll likely be trying to compensate during the next one. Unfortunately, this can actually work against you. Large portions can be overwhelming for a toddler, especially one who is already being fussy.

Tip #2: *Let Them Pretend They Are on Masterchef Junior*

One cure for the mealtime blues involves allowing your child to help with meal prep. Turning your toddler into a tiny kitchen assistant can get them more interested in not only the eating process, but the cooking process as well. A child is naturally going to get more excited about eating a meal they have helped make. Of course, that means you may have to eat some ghastly concoctions (my son once whipped up a wet bread and baloney sandwich for me with a syrup glaze. He's very lucky there isn't a toddler version of Yelp.) Letting your child cook also taps into their natural interest in the world around them; it can also help them feel more in control of something that may have previously overwhelmed them. In addition, they will be eager to imitate, so the more they see you cooking in the kitchen, the more they'll want to throw on their tiny apron!

Tip#3: *Keep Meal Times Regular and Consistent*

While repeating the same ingredients or foods can become tedious to your toddler, regular mealtimes are essential. Children tend to thrive in an environment of predictability, and the more comfortably they settle into the idea of eating at certain times, the more adventurous they'll be in trying new foods. Therefore, try to have a set time for breakfast, lunch, and dinner, hitting those preset meals with as much consistency as possible. Of course, eating at the same time every day isn't always possible, but do what you can to get your child in a rhythm. You can also schedule a snack time between breakfast and lunch and another between lunch and dinner. While satisfying a picky eater with junk food could be tempting, it's best to keep these snacks healthy and filling. That way, you won't be dealing with a hungry child as you are cooking their next big meal.

Tip #4: *As Always, It Pays to Have Patience.*

I'll say something right now about patience in parenting: certain situations just aren't going to be fair. Your child will be running around, impatiently shrieking for chicken nuggets, and you just have to take a deep breath and force a smile. All parents know that children are experts at playing jump rope with our last nerves, and when we are talking about a critical situation like their nutrition, that nerve may already be worn thin. But, as with almost every stage of parenthood, patience is key. It can take as many as 20 exposures to a new food before your toddler becomes familiar with it and will start to take nibbles. So stick with it, keep putting those greens on their plate, and (hopefully) they will eventually take a bite.

Tip #5: *When it Comes to Healthy Food, Be a Master of Disguise*

Here's another excellent way to get your child past a picky eating phase: Trick them! Okay, that may sound awful, but it's not actually as nefarious as it sounds. There are ways to transform traditionally boring and healthy foods into snacks that can entice adults and children alike. Let's take celery, for example. You'll be hard-pressed to find a child who will initially enjoy the crunchy texture, watery taste, and overall construction-material-like quality of celery (clearly, I'm not a huge fan myself.) But, by adding a few other ingredients, you can convert this bland and earthy vegetable into a treat your children will ask for over and over. You've likely heard of the classic "ants on a log," but I've added a few optional ingredients you can play around with if your child is extra picky.

Customizable Ants on a Log Recipe

Ingredients:

- 4 stalks of celery

- ½ cup of your favorite nut or seed butter (I recommend almond or peanut butter)

- ¼ cup dried fruit (raisins, cranberries, or craisins are all excellent)

- ¼ cup granola (to give the treat a bit more of a crunch)

- Drizzle of honey (for extra sweetness without too much extra sugar. **Note:** do not give your children honey if they are under the age of 1.)

- Sprinkle of flax or chia seeds (which can provide antioxidants, fiber, and other nutrients)

Instructions:

To start, cut and wash your "logs" (i.e., celery stalks) and pat them dry with a paper towel. Cut each stalk into 3-inch long pieces, and carefully spoon your butter selection into the hollow U-shape of the celery stalks. After that, you can sprinkle your granola over the top of the butter and dot it with your "ants" (whatever dried fruit you choose.) From there, you can drizzle your honey and sprinkle your seeds. Remember, you can remove or change out any of these ingredients if your child doesn't seem interested. You'd be surprised, though, I've brought this snack to many gatherings, and not once have I come home with anything but an empty plate!

The "Don'ts" of Picky Eating

Just like there are things you should do in the kitchen, there are a few things you absolutely should **not** do. Your toddler is forming associations with food that they may carry throughout their lives, so it's essential to avoid the pitfalls that many parents face when it comes to nutritional pickiness.

Don't *Try to Force Feed Your Toddler*

When there is an obstacle in your way, it may seem logical to just push as hard as possible until the path opens up. While this may work for getting into your frozen front door during a blizzard, the plan really falls apart when it comes to feeding your toddler. Forcing your child to eat can turn the dinner table into a battlefield, causing your little one to associate certain foods with stress (or the thought of mealtime altogether). I understand you worked hard to make that meal, and tossing it in the fridge (or worse, the trash) may cause your blood to boil. But making your child clean their plate will create more resistance later on, trust me. Instead, make sure your toddler feels comfortable and in control of the situation as much as possible. They'll begin to warm up to the food on their own, and best of all, they will think it was their idea all along!

Don't *Use Food As a Punishment*

Speaking of forcing someone to eat, this can be taken even further in the wrong direction by using food as a punishment. If you're like me, your parents probably did this at one time or another. I remember one particular evening when I finally took a stand against the broccoli on my plate. I told my mother that I wasn't going to eat those weird little trees, not now, not ever. Little did I know it, but my act of rebellion would end in a 4-hour standoff between me and those little florets. I was told that until I finished that food, I wasn't allowed to leave the table. So I held out as long as I could (4 hours is at least nine years in toddler time). Eventually, I choked down the long-cold handful of veggies, but to this day, I get Vietnam-style flashbacks whenever I see broccoli on a plate.

Because of this negative association, I avoid broccoli whenever I can, despite many people telling me it is their favorite vegetable. Your toddler will be no different; while using food as a punishment may work one time, you'll likely create a lifetime disdain for whatever happens to be on their plate at that time.

Don't *Compare Your Children to Others*

Like with potty training and so many other milestones, your toddler will progress at different rates than other children. While your friends or other parents may be bragging about the healthy foods their kids are gobbling up, it's possible that your little tyke just hasn't got there quite yet. Stay persistent, consistent, and patient, and eventually, your child should begin to acquire a more diverse palate. Of course, if they struggle for too long, you may want to talk to more experienced parents or a nutritionist. It's also possible they are dealing with an illness, and bringing them to their pediatrician could be helpful.

From Soup to Sleep, Let's Breakdown Bedtime

Now that you know a bit more about how to win the battle of the broccoli, it's time to talk about something just as crucial as nutrition: sleep. Proper sleep is essential for the development and health of your toddler, and in Chapter 4, we'll discuss the effects too little sleep can have on your child, as well as some strategies to tackle sleep-related issues.

Dad Hacks from Chapter 3

Picky Eating Hack #1: Become a Food Wizard. Try changing the shape or texture of certain foods to get your child through a period of picky eating. You can blend fruits and veggies into a shake, use cookie cutters to make fun shapes, or even tell stories that make your child believe certain foods are "magic."

Picky Eating Hack #2: The Trojan Broccoli. In addition to letting your children know about any changes you are making to the food, you can also sneak some nutrition into meals they otherwise like. For example, if they like spaghetti but hate carrots and bell peppers, blend them up into your marinara sauce.

Picky Eating Hack #3: Mealtime Mirroring. Your children look up to you, and in many cases will copy or mimic your behavior. Use this to your advantage when dealing with a picky eater. If you make a big show of eating a plate of spinach, saying how delicious it is and even claiming they can't have any, watch how quickly your children will ask for a plate of their own.

Picky Eating Hack #4: Make Dinner an Event. It's easy to get caught up in the chaos of daily life, but try to make dinner a family event. While it may not be possible every night, whenever you can sit everyone down and talk about your day. If your toddler sees everyone smiling, laughing, and eating, they will likely do the same.

Picky Eating Hack #5: Tiny Toddler Greenthumb. If you have the space, you could also get your child involved in some gardening. Growing healthy fruits and vegetables together is not only a great way to bond, but it can make your toddler more connected (and more inclined to eat) the food they grow.

Chapter 4

Slumber Struggles: Strategies You Can Use to Solve Sleep-related Issues

According to the American Academy of Pediatrics, **25 to 50 percent** of children are affected by sleep problems at some point during their early lives. Considering sleep's vital role in a child's development, this statistic may cause you some concern. I can tell you from personal experience having a toddler that can't seem to doze off can play havoc with a parent's mind.

My daughter, ever the electric ball of energy, had issues getting proper rest in her younger days. These problems only intensified when we tried to move her from a crib to a regular-sized bed. Many a night, she would leave her room, and I would find her shuffling through her toy box at 2 in the morning. Naturally, I would have to stay up to make sure she was okay, which meant I was a zombie at work the next day. This vicious cycle continued to the point where I felt I only had two options: Discover the cure for toddler insomnia or surrender to the madness of sleep deprivation. Fortunately, we got through that rough patch and got back to a healthier sleep pattern.

During these sleepless nights I found that, while sleep problems can seem overwhelming, there are plenty of solutions you can implement. To start, let's talk about what exactly makes sleep so crucial to your child's healthy growth.

What Makes Sleep So Important for Toddlers

Good sleep can have numerous physical, emotional, and developmental effects on your little one. Some of the ways that adequate sleep can help include:

- **Promoting Better Development, Learning, and Memory:** While it may appear that your little one is simply resting peacefully in dreamland, their body is actually hard at work growing key areas of the brain and body. Not only are growth hormones released during sleep, but the memories of the day are sorted and encoded within the brain. This helps your toddler remember what they've learned and build upon those experiences to reach new developmental milestones. Proper rest will also give them the energy and attention span to approach new subjects effectively; without it, they are likely to struggle throughout the day.

- **Supporting Their Immune System:** Adequate sleep acts as a supercharger for your child's immune system, bolstering their ability to fight off illness and disease. Your toddler is probably running around the playground, touching every surface they can, and interacting with other children who are most likely covered in germs. Good sleep can help defend their bodies against these microscopic marauders, keeping them healthy and happy so they can get through the day safely.

- **Facilitating Better Moods and Appetite Regulation:** Nobody likes a cranky child, and a lack of sleep can turn your bundle of joy into a barrel of anger. Good sleep can keep those tantrums at bay and make your child more likely to follow your instructions. Proper rest will also keep their appetite in check; failing to get adequate sleep can cause a hormonal imbalance that could lead to lower satiety and overeating.

- **Aiding in Tissue Growth and Repair:** Remember those nighttime growth hormones we talked about before? Well, not only do they help your child grow up big and strong, but they also aid in repairing vital tissue. A high-energy toddler is likely going to get dinged up every once in a while. Whether it's a skinned knee, a scuffed elbow, or a small cut, sleep gives your child's body the ability to quickly heal tissue and recover from injury.

- **Reducing Accident and Injury Risk:** So what's better than fixing injuries quickly? Not having them at all! A well-rested child is less likely to have accidents, and adequate sleep will mean your toddler is more coordinated, more alert, and less prone to moments of clumsiness. Making sure they have a regular bedtime and get their beauty rest could mean a lot fewer scrapes and tears.

3 Signs That Your Toddler May Not Be Getting the Sleep They Need

Sleepy Sign #1: *They Struggle to Wake Up and Get Drowsy During the Day*

Well-rested kids will usually wake up ready to take on the day, while a tired toddler will struggle to get up in the morning. Not only that, but a sleep-deprived toddler may doze off repeatedly throughout the day. For adults, this can usually be solved with a few extra cups of coffee during the day; for children, this drowsiness can be a signal they need better sleep.

Sleepy Sign #2: *They Seem Moodier and Can't Focus*

Because sleep is essential for mood regulation, a sleepy child is likely to go through a series of mood swings. If you notice that your toddler can fly into a tantrum at a moment's notice or just generally seems more irritable, that may mean they aren't getting enough sleep at night. You also may see that your child is struggling to complete specific tasks, even ones that they had previously mastered. This is because your child's energy is taken up fighting fatigue, so they don't have much left over for problem-solving, learning, or concentrating.

Sleepy Sign #3: *You Notice Changes in Their Appetite, Digestion, and Immune System Response*

Sleep deprivation can increase ghrelin levels, a hormone that can cause your toddler to feel hungrier and overeat. This hunger hormone works in tandem with another hormone called leptin: A lack of adequate sleep lowers leptin levels, which makes a person feel less satiated by meals. Digestion will also be hindered if a child does not get enough sleep, and as a result, your toddler may experience acid reflux or constipation. But of all the affected systems, the most dire may be the immune system. Sleep produces cytokines, which reduce the occurrence of infection and inflammation. Think of cytokines like a little army fighting to protect your toddler; if that army doesn't get proper sleep, they can't fight!

How Much Sleep Does a Toddler Need?

How much naptime your little tyke needs will depend mainly on their age. Let's look at a few different age ranges and what their sleep schedule will look like.

12 Months to 24 Months *(1 to 2 Years Old)*

Between the ages of 1 and 2, your toddler will likely need **11 to 14 hours** of sleep a day. While this does include a smattering of glorious and tranquil naps throughout the day, you'll notice that their sleep cycles will start to shift and become more established. With each passing month between 1 and 2, you'll see fewer interruptions in their nightly sleep and fewer naps during the daytime. This nap volume will only decrease as they get older.

24 to 36 Months *(2 to 3 Years Old)*

As your child passes the 24-month mark, their nap count will slowly drop until they are only having a single nap per day. This will coincide with a stable nocturnal pattern of slumber, which usually consists of between **10 and 13 hours** of steady sleep. Any hours they don't get at night will (hopefully) be made up for during the day, with 1-3 hour naps often occurring during the afternoon.

36 to 48 Months *(3 to 4 Years Old)*

That single nap will probably hold on until your toddler gets close to 3 years old, but this varies from child to child. Your toddler may need a bit more sleep to stay smiling, and that's totally fine; as long as they aren't sleeping to the point where fatigue or sickness is a concern, naps are perfectly healthy. Your child will need around the same amount of sleep during this time as well, with **10 to 12** or **10 to 13 hours** being the norm.

Throw Out That Crib, It's Time for the "Big Bed"

As time progresses, you'll notice that your toddler may be climbing out of their baby bed or getting too big to fit in it comfortably. This can mean they are ready to leave the confines of their crib and move on to a regular bed. Many children transition into a larger sleeping space between 1 ½ and 3 and a ½ years old, though it's important not to rush them if they aren't ready. A good place to start is by letting them select their new bed, as this can make them more comfortable with the transition. For example, my son went with the classic race car bed, while my daughter chose one with a "Little Mermaid" theme.

Once you have the bed set up, get them acquainted with it by spending time doing regular activities around and in it. This can mean playing their favorite board games, reading books, watching movies, or taking naps. As your child spends more time doing familiar activities in their new bed, they will start to associate positive feelings with this new sleeping space. Once they start to sleep in the bed more, give them positive encouragement and let them know you are proud of them.

What To Do If Your Toddler Is Struggling to Reach Dreamland

Remember that frustration you felt when your toddler wouldn't eat? Well, you will likely feel the same level of stress when your child can't sleep. This stress can be twofold because not only is your child not getting the sleep they need, but you probably aren't either. So is there any way to win the sleepytime struggle? Fortunately, yes. I've assembled a few tactics you can use to get your toddler snoozin' and cruisin' toward dreamland.

1. **Create a Consistent Bedtime Routine:** While kids may seem chaotic, they tend to strive when you give them structure. A good bedtime routine consisting of calming activities like a bath, reading, and soothing music can all help your toddler wind down at the end of a big day. If your child is anxious about sleeping, you can also use a technique called the "second goodnight." This involves letting them know you will be back in 15 minutes to say goodnight again, which will relax them. As you push this follow-up goodnight further back, you'll notice they will often be asleep by the time you check on them. Eventually, you won't need to do it at all!

2. **Optimize Their Sleep Environment:** If your toddler's room is hot, loud, or bright, they will likely have a tough time getting to sleep. Getting their sleep environment dialed in will take some time, as every child has unique needs. You generally want the room on the cooler side, with the best range often sitting between 63 and 68 degrees Fahrenheit. If your child isn't comfortable with complete darkness, a red-colored nightlight can offer them comfort without producing the sleep interference of blue light. For noise, you'll want to try to keep your home as quiet as possible at night. If it isn't possible to have complete silence, a fan or white noise machine can cover up any sonic disruptions that may drift through your home.

3. **Regular Wake-ups and Positive Reinforcement:** Having a regular wake-up time and morning routine is just as essential as having a consistent nighttime one, and getting your toddler up at the same time every day can dramatically improve their circadian rhythms. One great way to do this is with a wake-up clock, which can gradually increase the brightness in their room and use soft chimes to raise them

from their slumber. You can also use rewards or stickers to encourage your child if they successfully stay in their bed all night or use techniques like the "Sleep Fairy." Similar to the Tooth Fairy, the Sleep Fairy gives children a small prize or toy if they sleep in their beds for a certain number of days. However you choose to structure your routine, make sure to keep it fun!

What Should I Do If My Toddler Repeatedly Leaves Their Bed?

Even if you do everything right, your child may still treat their bed like a prison and attempt to escape at any chance possible. In these cases, it's best to sit them down and explain just how important sleep is. If they still rebel, you may have to put your foot down and tell them that bedtime isn't a choice. While you still want to ensure they are safe, setting boundaries and letting them self-soothe when they call out for your attention at night can be helpful. If you are anxious about doing this, you can have a baby monitor in the room to ensure their cries are only for attention and not emergencies.

You may also want to give them some kind of security item, like a blanket or toy. One trick to helping this work is to tell them that the blanket or toy has "magic sleep powers" and can help guide them to dreamland. Security items are a great way to increase your toddler's comfort, especially during the transition period between their crib and bed. This, in conjunction with a nightlight, can really help a child feel safe in their bedroom, making them less likely to leave.

If nighttime issues persist, you may want to talk to a pediatrician or sleep specialist. I can't overstate how important sleep is, and if disruptions continue for too long, they can start to harm your child or restrict their development. So don't be afraid to contact your doctor and seek out further assistance with this issue if it continues.

How to Handle Nightmares and Night Terrors

Leaving the bed at night is one thing, and it is sometimes appropriate to let your child deal with a mild level of bedtime discomfort on their own. However, nightmares and night terrors are another thing altogether; these instances can be especially terrifying for your toddler and, left unaddressed, may cause them to create long-lasting negative associations with their new bed and bedtime in general.

So what is the difference between nightmares and night terrors? Well, nightmares are often frightening dreams that cause your child to wake up in a state of panic. While nightmares can come about for seemingly no reason, they can also be more frequent in periods of stress (like the transition to a new bed), happen after traumatic events or while adjusting to new medications, or even occur due to a simple lack of adequate sleep.

To help your toddler avoid or deal with nightmares, you'll want to start by reassuring them that they are safe. Ask them what they saw in their dream and tell them that none of it is real, that you are close by, and everything will be alright. You can also look for hints within the dream itself to try to discern the source of their stress and avoid exposing them to any scary or violent content before they go to sleep.

Night terrors, on the other hand, are a non-REM sleep-related disturbance. These can involve your child reacting physically despite still being unconscious. They can scream, kick, thrash, and appear as though they are awake, but in many cases, they won't remember the incident when they wake up in the morning.

Dealing with night terrors is a bit different than nightmares, as you don't want to wake them up if you can help it. Waking up the child can be traumatic, leading to confusion and even prolonging a night terror occurrence. Instead, make sure your child isn't close to any objects that can harm them while they have their reaction; if they do wake up, comfort them and let them know that everything is fine.

Transitioning Into the Terrible Twos

A lack of sleep can make a child (or adult) of any age cranky, but what if your child seems to be angry no matter what? If that's the case, it's possible you are dealing with a period of time commonly referred to as the "Terrible Twos," a period of time in your toddler's development often associated with defiance, resistance, and overall emotional turmoil. In our next chapter, we'll talk about what you can expect during this time and the best ways to deal with a combative child.

Dad Hacks from Chapter 4

Sleep Hack #1: Let Them Get Familiar With Their New Bed. The more your child spends time in their room with their new bed, the faster they will want to leave their crib and hop in. Letting them choose the bed itself and sheets, while also planning activities in their room, can all help them get comfortable and ready to sleep comfortably.

Sleep Hack #2: Offer a Late-Night Snack. While a big meal can reduce sleep quality, a light nighttime snack can help your toddler fall asleep with ease. Some good food choices include yogurt, bananas, and whole-grain crackers, which contain nutrients or amino acids that can help produce valuable sleep-regulation hormones.

Sleep Hack #3: Chart Your Child's Pillow Progress. Children respond well to visual stimuli, and having a chart with stickers and reasonable milestones can help them feel as though they are progressing further in their bedtime journey. Every night your child successfully gets to bed on time or stays in their bed all night, placing a sticker on their chart. You can even let them choose the stickers to further increase their motivation.

Sleep Hack #4: Stories Go a Long Way. Reading a story at night to your child is a time tested relaxation technique, but you can go a step further by creating tales that involve your child and their sleep struggles. Craft a story with a main character who is battling sleep-related monsters and address any anxieties your toddler may be having through your narrative. This can help them process their problems and make them realize they aren't the first child to go through this problem.

Sleep Hack #5: Don't forget the Quiet Game. It may be well worn territory at this point, but the classic "Quiet Game" can help a rambunctious child calm down at the end of the day. Your child may want to run around and yell, but once the quiet game starts, their natural inclination to play will be triggered. This quiet can be accompanied by gentle music or white noise to help them calmly drift off.

Chapter 5

Find Shelter! The Terrible Two Tornado is Here

I've traveled through the land of the Terrible Twos a few times now, and I can tell you, it never gets easier. From thrown toys to splattered soup, cleaning up a toddler's mess while they berate you is enough to drive the most patient parent crazy. A lot of the time, the habits our toddlers fall into don't even make sense. I can recall a phase my son went through where he would methodically take his toys one by one and throw them out into the muddy yard. When I dutifully retrieved them, he would burst into tears and begin his toy evacuation once again. I can tell you that, on more than one occasion, I had to walk outside and have a tantrum of my own. The point is, you will get frustrated during this time, and that's okay. The best way to get through the Terrible Twos is to understand what is happening, when it's beginning, and how to deal with it.

The Terrible Twos Phenomenon: What is it?

Starting around year two, you may notice that your formerly joyful and exuberant little toddler has had a drastic attitude change. They begin to fly into tantrums with no warning, their favorite word becomes "no," and they may even start to wear a tiny leather jacket and smoke candy cigarettes! (This last part isn't true, but you get the picture.) Your little rebel can shift their mood on a dime and is more likely to test the boundaries of what they can get away with. With the combination of stress and frustration many feel during this time period, it's no wonder why it's been labeled as "terrible."

So what causes this phenomenon? Well, part of the issue lies in just how rapidly your toddler is changing during this time. Their ability to speak, move about, and understand the world around them is evolving at a dizzying pace, so it's more than likely they are frustrated and confused. With so many fires burning at once, it's easy for there to be an explosion every once in a while.

In addition to developmental changes, your child is also learning the value of autonomy and independence. As they begin to move around more and get a feel for things, they'll want to challenge the restrictions that had previously hemmed them in. Unfortunately, part of this exploration can mean they'll try to assert that independence in ways that clash with your wishes. These clashes can be further exacerbated by the emotional rollercoaster that their feelings are going through.

Toddlers don't mean to fly off the handle, but because they are so new to the concept of emotions, it's understandable they will lose control now and then. These outbursts are made worse by the fact that your toddler hasn't quite grasped the ability to communicate correctly. Imagine how frustrating it would be to have feelings you want to talk about, but you don't know how to express yourself meaningfully. Tantrums, while extreme, function as a way to let others know they are frustrated with their situation.

3 Signs You've Entered the Terrible Twos

There are a few signs to recognize that the Terrible Twos have arrived. These often include:

- **Barrage of Backtalk:** As your toddler develops their language skills, you may start to notice more opposition or whining when they're asked to do something. This is all part of the resistance and rebellion that underlies the Terrible Twos; fueled by rapidly shifting emotions, your child will not be afraid to tell you if they don't like dinner, an activity, or a particular person.

- **The Mini-Stuntman:** Part curiosity, part independence, all danger. Your child's increased mobility will allow them to explore to their heart's content, and their budding desire for freedom will lead them to run off in search of new stimulation. While they may have upgraded acceleration, their braking will need time to catch up, and you can expect quite a few scrapes and accidents.

- **Push it to the Limit:** Your toddler is going to start toeing the line and seeing what they can get away with, starting with taking possession of objects that probably aren't theirs. Even if they've learned about sharing, this time period will be filled with them taking things and yelling out "mine," much to your chagrin. This isn't the only boundary they will test either: public meltdowns, biting, and breaking things are all on the table. Get ready to experience the full gambit of bad behavior!

Terrible Tantrums and Magnificent Meltdowns: How to Handle Them

One of the defining characteristics of these terrible times is the classic temper tantrum, an uncontrolled outburst accompanied by screaming, stomping, and even more theatrical displays of emotionality. Tantrums don't care where they pop up, whether that be in the grocery store, the background of your work Zoom call, or in the middle of a wedding ceremony. Luckily, there are ways to deal with these emotional explosions.

Access Your Inner Zen Buddha

Remember, toddlers love to emulate your behavior; if they see you freak out when they go into a tantrum, that will only make things worse. When a meltdown erupts, it's essential to take a few deep breaths and remain calm. Gently talk to your child and tell them you understand what they are going through. "I can tell that you are really frustrated right now, little fella. That seems tough; I'm sorry." Your child will see your calm demeanor and reassuring tone and (hopefully) gain some self-awareness of the situation.

Time for a Distraction

Never underestimate the power of a perfectly placed smoke-bomb-style diversion. If your child is getting upset, try to identify the cause. Is it because they want a toy in the store and can't have it? Is it because you've taken away a bag of candy they were trying to eat in one giant bite like a snake? Is it because their favorite sports team lost the Super Bowl? Whatever the reason, try to change their focus or activity. If possible, give them a few choices to make, as this can activate the logical parts of their mind instead of the emotional ones. In addition, letting them choose helps them feel more in control, which can further hold their attention.

Be Firm, But Fair

It's essential that you stick to the boundaries you set and don't waver in the face of your wailing child. Believe me, it's tough, especially if you are in a place where your child's tantrum is causing you immediate embarrassment. I've personally dealt with a candy-related tantrum in the middle of a funeral, during which I frantically gave my child enough sugar to put down an elephant. Unfortunately, giving in to your child's demands will only set a precedent for the future. If you give in now, they'll know there is a threshold for your patience that they can break through. This means next time, they'll know exactly how long they need to cry before you'll give up. Of course, that doesn't mean you shouldn't reward them when they do well. If your child stops having a tantrum or avoids one altogether by communicating, make sure to praise them. Positive reinforcement is powerful and can help motivate your toddler next time they feel overwhelmed.

Tips to Help Dads Survive the Storm

Poet Robert Frost famously said, "The best way out is always through." While we can't be sure he was talking about parenting, the quote describes the Terrible Twos perfectly: you can't get out of this; you can only go through it. Fortunately, there are plenty of ways you can endure this period of time and even have fun while doing it! Here are a few tips you can use as a dad to survive the storm.

Tip #1: *Always Find the Funny*

It can be easy to get down or melancholy during difficult moments in your parenting journey. I remember one gloomy period when my daughter was a toddler where, no matter how many times we asked her not to, she would continuously draw all over the walls of our house. We provided her with art supplies, but she just used those on the walls as well. Then, we hid the crayons, pens, paint, and any drawing implement she could get her hands on; still, this bite-sized Banksy continued on her graffiti rampage.

Eventually, at our wit's end, we compromised; we provided washable markers and selected a specific space on the wall for her to draw on until she got through that phase. I remember after one weekend of diligently scrubbing away, my wife surprised me with a gift. As I opened it, I immediately started laughing; it was a photo of one of my daughter's more extravagant pieces framed as though it were a piece of fine art. I still have that framed photo sitting in my office, and I can't help but smile every time I look at it.

Joking around or making light of certain events doesn't minimize the importance of your role as a parent. Instead, humor can serve as a valuable stress-release valve, taking a bit of the pressure out of a situation that may be close to boiling over. Remember, your toddler is also stressed out during this time. They will be facing obstacles in their development that will seem overwhelming; to make things easier, smile and laugh along with them when they make a mistake. Being overly serious or strict will only make things more challenging, and sometimes, a good laugh can help encourage your child to try again. So whether you are scrubbing crayons or cleaning up spaghetti, take a second to smile and take a mental snapshot of the moment. Believe me, one day, you will miss even the low moments of early parenthood.

Tip #2: *Exercise is an Ally, Not an Enemy*

While getting your kids worked up may seem counterintuitive, exercise is actually one of the best ways to burn off the excess energy coursing through your toddler's veins. Not only that but regular physical activity can:

- Encourage exploration

- Strengthen your toddler's body

- Help them learn balance and coordination

- Allow them to get better sleep

- Assist them in regulating their mood

- Improve their sleep

The key here is variety. You want to introduce your toddler to a wide range of environments and activities. These environments can be basic, like a play place set up in your backyard, but should also include other areas like beaches and parks. Organizing a trip somewhere outdoors is also a good time to encourage socialization, as you can invite other parents and children to come along. Your toddlers can dart around while you supervise and talk to other adults about their experiences. Share any tips you have about your own Terrible Twos journey, and ask them what advice they may have for you.

Exercise isn't only helpful for your toddler either. The Terrible Twos is stressful, and physical activity is one of the best natural stress relievers available. Not only that, but exercise can give you a wide range of benefits like:

- Improved heart health

- Relief from the symptoms of anxiety and depression

- Improved cognitive function

- Easier weight management

- Boosted immune function

- Reduced risk of chronic disease

Tip #3: *Take Some Time For Yourself*

While your toddler should be the primary focus of your life right, that doesn't mean your health and identity don't still matter. Fatherhood can be one of the most rewarding experiences in life, but it can also be exceedingly exhausting. Being a parent is a marathon, not a spring, and taking some time for self-care is essential.

Part of this self-care should be a healthy and balanced diet. Fruits, veggies, lean proteins, and plenty of water; you'll need the fuel to keep up with your little ball of lightning as they ricochet around the room, and eating well will allow you to do just that. This is easier said than done, as I have personally been guilty of eating leftover mac and cheese or dinosaur chicken nuggets at 2 am after a tough day. One way to ensure you get good food and still have time to take care of everything else is by meal prepping. Plan your meals out for the week, and prep and cook all of your food once you have a free hour or two. You can portion each meal out into reheatable containers; that way, instead of going through a fast food drive-thru or buying one of those sad rolling hotdogs at the gas station, you can pop a delicious and balanced meal right into the microwave or oven.

You'll also want to try your best to do something nice for yourself (or you and your spouse). That could mean getting a babysitter and doing date night, watching a game on Sundays, going for a bike ride while listening to an audiobook, or any other activity you find refreshing and relaxing. Remember, engaging in self-care doesn't mean you are being selfish. If you burn the candle at both ends and neglect yourself, you won't be able to give your best to your family.

While It Isn't Fun, Discipline is Necessary

Even after you pass through the Terrible Twos, there will still be times your toddler tests the boundaries, acts out, or melts down. While no one enjoys doing it, discipline is a necessary part of parenting. In our next chapter, we'll discuss why discipline is important, techniques to discipline your child with compassion, and what not to do when disciplining your toddler.

Dad Hacks from Chapter 5

Terrible Two's Hack #1: Keep a Snack-Attack Solution With You. While tantrums can be caused by a variety of things, one of the most common culprits is hunger. Keeping a quick and healthy snack with you to give to your toddler can help stop a rampage before it starts.

Terrible Two's Hack #2: Drain Their Batteries. Toddlers have a wealth of energy that would make the Energizer Bunny jealous, and too much excess left at the end of the day can mean tantrums and sleeplessness. Find a few different physical activities they like to do and give them the opportunity to tire themselves out, especially on days they seem extra grumpy.

Terrible Two's Hack #3: Distractions Are Your Friend. Find a toy, book, or any other object that tends to calm your child down and keep it with you wherever you go. When you see the beginnings of a tantrum bubbling up, you can use this special item as an antidote to quell your toddler's rage.

Terrible Two's Hack #4: Schedule Self-Care. While you likely can't pick an entire day of the week to focus on yourself, try to find a couple of hours per week or a whole day once a month you can dedicate entirely to self-care. Do whatever you want during this time, clearing your mind of any worries relating to your children for a brief period. This can help you recharge and focus better once you return.

Terrible Two's Hack #5: Laugh Off the Little Stuff. Look, things are going to go wrong. That's just what being a parent is all about. But it's important to give your toddler (and yourself) a bit of leeway. Joke about mishaps when they occur, comfort your child, and let them know that they'll do better next time.

Chapter 6

Dealing with Discipline: Techniques to Teach Your Toddler Consequences with Compassion

I've always struggled with discipline throughout my parenting journey, and I don't think I'm alone. We love our kids and want them to be happy and smiling every moment of every day, but the fact is, there are times when children ignore the rules and cause problems. I shared a few examples in the last chapter of mishaps that happened during the terrible twos, but unfortunately, there will be incidents during all parts of childhood.

We can see this in action with my daughter, who often had trouble with boundaries regarding treats and candy, especially jelly beans. I remember the first moment I gave her a tiny package of those colorful sugary little devils, not knowing I had essentially just given a chain smoker her first cigarette. Almost immediately, we had to limit how many jellybeans my daughter could eat. Of course, she disregarded this new rule with lightning speed. After one particular bean rationing, I remember her snagging the entire bag when I wasn't looking. It wasn't until later, when I found her in her room in the throws of an intense and uncomfortable sugar high, that I decided she had to face the consequences. Despite my frustration, I took a deep breath and approached the situation with care and understanding.

"Sweetie, remember when I told you that eating too many jelly beans would make you sick?" She nodded her head; her pupils dilated with the kilos of sugar pulsing through her veins. We talked about what happened, and I explained that her discomfort was a result of the natural consequences of stepping over that particular boundary.

The next time we had jelly beans in the house, there was a moment where I saw her struggling to decide how much to take. But alas, she recalled the last time she had binged and chose only to take a small portion. This perfectly illustrates how the right kind of discipline can be effective and why discipline can often be helpful instead of harmful.

What's the Deal with Discipline Anyway?

While discipline is easily one of the least pleasant things that a parent has to do, it's a necessary evil with crucial benefits. Proper discipline is one of the secret ingredients of future success; sure, it may be a spicier ingredient, but it can provide our children a roadmap of boundaries, safety guidelines, and give life a consistent, predictable rhythm. Not only that, but discipline can also be instrumental in facilitating numerous components of healthy development. Here are some of the ways that discipline can help your toddler in the present and future.

- **Laying Down the Boundary Lines:** I genuinely believe that a toddler invented the saying "rules were meant to be broken." They seem to find any opportunity to cross the lines you've set out. The key is to set out clear expectations of what happens when a line is crossed. Discipline instills the values of responsibility and accountability, teaching your toddler that every action comes with a consequence.

- **Supporting Development and Growth:** Proper discipline has the power to fuel your toddler's emotional and social development. Once they begin to see the results of rule-breaking, they'll start to build up a sense of self-control, empathy, and respect for others. Consequences will also teach them to expand their decision-making skills; if they experience a negative outcome from an action, they'll probably decide to avoid taking that action in the future.

- **Keeping Them Safe:** Not only can discipline help your toddler understand how to navigate the social challenges of life, but it can also be a lifesaver, literally! If the boundaries you set concern potential risks and dangers (like "don't stick metal forks into electrical outlets, you'll explode"), your toddler will begin to associate risky actions with dire consequences. This mindset can keep them safe when they are young and could be vital later in life.

- **Consistency and Comfort:** Despite their innate rebellious streaks, toddlers thrive on consistency. A set of definite rules gives them a sense of predictability, fostering a safe environment for learning and growing. This paves the way for them to adapt to environments with similar expectations later on, like school or work.

- **Instilling Respect and Values:** Compassionate discipline is one of the building blocks cornerstone of respect and strong values. Disciplining your child when they disregard the boundaries you've created will teach them to respect authority and the feelings of others. These skills will be useful throughout their childhood and well into adulthood, setting them up for more significant success and enabling them to become contributing members of society.

3 Tips to Keep Discipline Positive and Compassionate

Tip #1: *Try a "Time-in" Instead of "Time-out"*

I'm sure you are familiar with the old-school "time-out" technique, a discipline method synonymous with isolation and lack of emotional support. Unfortunately, this technique is often more unsettling than corrective. Instead of isolating your child, try to open a dialogue with them. With the "time-in" approach, you can help your toddler understand their mistake and process the emotions they might be feeling. It's essential to express how their actions made you feel as well, as this will help them foster empathy and understand the emotional consequences of breaking a rule.

Tip #2: *Take the Opportunity to Expand Their Problem-solving Skills*

When your toddler breaks a rule and is subsequently disciplined, they may be confused as to what is happening. Give your child the puzzle pieces of the situation by letting them know the rules they broke and explaining the consequences they are encountering. This can help engage their burgeoning problem-solving skills, creating connections in their brain between the action they took and the reaction after. It helps in these cases to keep rules and consequences consistent, so they can more easily understand why discipline is occurring. You can also use natural consequences to ensure they efficiently identify the cause-and-effect relationship of breaking boundaries. For example, if they refuse to eat their food and they later tell you they are hungry, explain to them that they are hungry because they spilled their dinner all over the floor!

Tip #3: *Give Positive Reinforcement and Model Good Behavior*

While your toddler will definitely have to face the music from time to time, a spoonful of sugar can help the medicine go down. Yes, some parts of the discipline process may seem negative, but it's also essential to acknowledge and reward good behavior. When your little tyke does a good job picking up their toys or finishing all their veggies, it's important to encourage them and celebrate their success.

You can add more positivity to the process by modeling the behavior you want to see in your child. For example, if you create a rule saying that food shouldn't be eaten in front of the TV, you wouldn't want your toddler to catch you scarfing down a meal with the game on in the background. Remember, your toddler is your biggest fan, and they want to be just like you. Sure, some rules are only meant for them, but trying to adhere to the same guidelines when they are around can be beneficial. That way, they can copy your behavior, feeling more "grown up" while also obeying the crucial rules you set.

What to Avoid When Disciplining Your Toddler

Good discipline isn't easy, and it can sometimes feel like you are juggling flaming torches while walking a shaky tightrope. You've got to maintain a good balance because one wrong move and things can go south pretty quickly. Now, I'm sure you have your own tricks of the trade when it comes to setting your kiddo straight, and that's perfectly fine within reason. However, some punishment paths can lead us straight into a thicket of negativity, potentially harming our little one's development.

Here are a few red flags to avoid when teaching your toddler about consequences:

- **Shaming and Humiliation:** We've all been there: you are at the end of your rope, pulling your hair out, and your stress levels are starting to tick up into the red. It's completely understandable to get frustrated occasionally, and while mistakes happen, you'll want to avoid insulting or humiliating your child at all costs. Calling your children names or belittling them can do significant damage to their self-esteem, which can cause them to struggle with mental health issues later on. Instead, be compassionate, encouraging, and understanding when you deploy discipline tactics. This is not only more effective, but you'll feel far better about yourself.

- **Physical Punishment:** It's unfortunate that so many generations before us used corporal punishment as a way to discipline their children. Like insults, physical punishment is ineffective and can dramatically increase the risk of mental health issues in your toddler. It also has the potential to ignite a tendency towards aggressive behavior that may persist into adulthood. Not only that, but physical consequences can cause deep resentment to build between you and your child, which will strain (and, in some cases, destroy) the parent-child relationship.

- **Isolation or Neglect:** We talked about time-outs before, and despite how commonly they're used, they are about as effective as a cruise ship made of sugar. There are two primary reasons this technique melts down and fails to achieve its intended purpose: one, it ignores the needs of your toddler, and two, it doesn't give them any actionable information. Your child will likely be confused and cry as they sit in a separate room or area, not understanding why they are in this distressing situation. Like other outdated punishment methods, this can lead to issues like emotional dysregulation later in their development.

- **Sky-High Expectations and Fickle Consequences:** Jumping between being as soft as a marshmallow one day and strict another as a drill sergeant the next can give your child a severe case of mental whiplash. Changing things around too much can make it hard for your toddler to get comfortable and learn the rules, increasing the chance that they will accidentally step out of line. Expecting your toddler to keep up with frequent boundary changes is just not feasible. It's essential to remember their current capabilities when creating rules or setting expectations. This can help you both avoid frustration and give your toddler the environment they need to grow (a topic discussed in depth below.)

- **Using Fear as a Teaching Tool:** Overreacting to a particular behavior or threatening your child with harm is an awful way to ensure they obey the rules, even if it may seem effective in the short term. Over time, scare tactics will wear on your child and cause deep emotional scars that may never go away. It can also cause them to lose trust in you; they may stop seeing you as a protector and instead start to view you as a tyrant.

How to Set Age-Appropriate Expectations and Create Reasonable Consequences

Navigating the labyrinth of discipline is all about understanding the lay of the land. Basically, it helps to know what developmental stage your child is in; that way, you can tailor expectations and consequences to match their current abilities. A discipline strategy that works well for a one-year-old might fall flat on its face for a three-year-old. To simplify this, I've separated toddler age groups into two camps below and listed some reasonable expectations and consequences you can use with each.

1st Age Group: **Toddlers Aged 1-2 Years**

- **Reasonable Expectations to Set:** At this age, your toddlers are tiny scientists, experimenting and interacting with various things in the world to see what the results are. They'll be poking, prodding, and grabbing anything they can get their little paws on, and to be honest, it's unrealistic to expect them to keep their hands to themselves at all times. Try to limit boundaries to the absolute essentials, barring them from touching objects or entering areas of your home that could directly endanger them. If they do slip up (and hoo boy, will they), remove them from the dangerous place quickly. Then, be patient and empathetic with your response. Children of this age are still getting the hang of things, and their attention spans are as short as their stubby little legs.

- **Effective Consequences to Utilize:** Speaking of short attention spans, a great compassionate consequence to use during this stage is redirection. Redirection involves using a toddler's limited attention span to your advantage. Picture this - you see your intrepid little explorer making a beeline for a restricted area. Instead of shouting out "NO!" try steering their attention towards an appropriate toy, object, or room. Once your child engages with the intended object, praise them to reinforce their good behavior. This can help you encourage good behavior while avoiding outright negativity.

73

2nd Age Group: Toddlers Aged 2-3 Years

- **Reasonable Expectations to Set:** As your toddler's language skills and sense of independence blossom, it will be easier for them to assess their own needs and desires. However, they may still be grappling with impulse control, which can lead them to struggle with sharing, taking turns, or avoiding testing certain boundaries. Craft boundaries that allow toddlers to flex their growing autonomy and let them "test the limits" in safe and respectful ways. Remember, while their abilities are rapidly expanding, they still have a long way to go; keep this in mind when creating rules and boundaries.

- **Effective Consequences to Utilize:** One consequence that works well with this age group is the "choice technique." This technique uses their rapidly increasing sense of independence as a way to encourage them to correct their behavior. Let's look at an example: Say your child refuses to share a toy with a sibling or friend, even after you've set a boundary concerning sharing. Ask them whether they would like to play with the toy alone in their room or whether they'd like to share the toy and continue to hang out with everyone else. In most cases, they will choose to share the toy; not only that, they will think this is a decision they came up with all on their own!

Discipline is an Important Step, But There is So Much More

Sure, discipline is a cornerstone in raising kind-hearted, empathetic, and respectful children. But remember, this is only one step in a parenting marathon that will involve many techniques and tactics. In our next chapter, we'll dive into building positive character traits, cultivating empathy and kindness, encouraging respect, and fostering a love of exploration and learning.

Dad Hacks from Chapter 6

Discipline Hack #1: Let Them Choose. As long as you keep the choices within certain limits, letting your child choose between two consequences can be a great way to empower your toddler, boost their decision-making stills, and still discipline them when they act out.

Discipline Hack #2: Natural Consequences Can Be Effective. Natural consequences involve letting a situation play out without artificially introducing discipline. For example, if your child won't wear rubber boots on a rainy day, their feet will get wet. This shows them cause-and-effect in a way that's easier to process.

Discipline Hack #3: Actively Listen and Understand. Traditional punishments often involve ignoring your child, which can be ineffective and even cruel. Talk your child through the consequences and explain to them the reasons they are being disciplined so they can behave correctly in the future.

Discipline Hack #4: Stay Consistent. Keeping boundaries consistent makes it easier for toddlers to understand what to do. This means they will be more likely to follow the rules and more comfortable exploring within their limits.

Discipline Hack #5: Create a "Happy Place." If all else fails, it helps to have an area of the home that can calm your child down. Fill a room or corner with pillows, blankets, books, or their favorite toys; whatever can give them a moment to breathe and regulate their emotions.

Chapter 7

Cultivating Character and Building Better Humans

Some days, parenthood can feel like you're the captain of a ship, steering through turbulent waters and feeling the fatigue of a long voyage. Meanwhile, your children are excited explorers, eager to crest the next wave and spot the next island. This natural curiosity will only grow as your children age and start to ask questions about the world around them. They'll want to know what things are, how to act in certain situations, and what it means to be a good person. As the captain of the U.S.S. Parenthood, it's your job to steer them toward the correct answers and safely get them to the Land of Adulthood.

One example I can think of from my own experience concerns the common conflict that surrounds toy sharing. I remember one particularly frustrating week when my son repeatedly abducted my daughter's stuffed rabbit and took it out in the yard. He would cover the poor bunny's white fur with dirt, then try to feed it baby carrots from the fridge before leaving it to soak in a mud bath. When I confronted him about this, he asked, "Why can't the rabbit be outside? Isn't that where they live?"

Rubbing my temples, I took a moment and breathed in deeply. First, I conceded that yes, some rabbits do indeed live outside. But this rabbit, his sister's rabbit, lived inside. Then, I told him that the rabbit was his sister's toy and that when he took it from her, it made her sad. It took some time, but I explained to him that the kind and respectful thing to do would be to wash the rabbit and return it with an apology. After realizing that he upset his sister, my son promptly washed the rabbit and returned it. When he did so, I made sure to tell him what a good job he had done. From then on, he let the rabbit live inside in peace, though he would occasionally remind me that rabbits should live outside, not inside (something that never fails to get a laugh out of my wife.)

Overall, the responsibility for instilling certain traits in your child will primarily be on your shoulders. While there are numerous qualities you can teach your toddler, I've narrowed it down to the five I believe will best prepare them for a successful and happy life.

5 Positive Character Traits to Set Your Child Up for Success

Like a parrot mimicking the sounds of a person talking, so will your children emulate the behavior they see around them. Toddlers are some of the world's best impressionists, and while they probably won't be getting on Saturday Night Live anytime soon, they will be performing their best celebrity impression of you every day. It's essential to remember this tendency for emulation when we teach them different values and traits. Try to serve as a shining example of the qualities you want to instill in your child; that way, they can pick them up easier and far more quickly.

Trait #1: *A Curious and Creative Mind*

Ahh, the magical world of "whys." I remember my daughter went through a phase where almost every one of her sentences began with the word why. "Why do dogs have tails?" "Why is grass green?" "Why can't I paint on the walls?" As parents, we can sometimes get annoyed when our children bombard us with a million "why" questions, but it's important not to brush these off. Their rapidly growing mind is trying to understand this wild world, and they will look to you as their guide. Each question is an opportunity to nourish their curiosity and imagination. Providing answers and having further conversations about specific topics can boost their passion for exploration and creativity.

You can also encourage creativity by introducing your child to different creative activities. This can mean playing music for them, helping them paint, or hyping them up to sing karaoke with you. This can plant the seeds that may someday grow into a magnificent tree of talent. Who knows, your toddler might become a famous music star or artist one day! That all starts by introducing them to creative outlets early on.

Trait #2: *A Kind and Empathetic Heart*

Our heart can be one of the best compasses in our lives, pointing us due north and ensuring we do the right thing. Teaching your children to listen to their hearts can be a great way to ensure they remain grateful, kind, and empathetic (all essential traits for your little future adult to have.) Guiding them through the nuances of this trait trio will make them far more likable and successful in life. You can do this by teaching them to say thank you when they are given something, encouraging them to see situations from the other person's perspective, and praising them when they are kind to others. This will ensure they make you proud and become the type of person who makes the world a better place.

Trait #3: *A Sense of Fairness and Integrity*

I always like to tell my kids that honesty is the best policy, even when no one is watching. Explain to your child what it means to "be fair" and show them why sticking to a set of values is important. An example you could use is the unguarded cookie jar; Even though they may be tempted to steal a cookie from the cookie jar when no one is looking, they'll feel better if they stay honest and do the right thing. They should also give others their fair share and avoid being greedy. Fairness and integrity are vital character traits to have, as these will allow your children to build stronger relationships and create a solid social network as they grow up.

Trait #4: *Responsibility and Self-Confidence*

Don't cry over spilled milk; clean it up! While accidents can be frustrating, they are also valuable teaching moments. Encouraging your children to own up to their actions will mold them into more responsible adults later in life. It will also make them feel more confident and secure in who they are. Explain to them that it's okay to make mistakes, but also explain that trying to lie or push the consequences onto someone else just won't cut it. The more they learn to take responsibility now, the more confident they'll be in the long run.

Trait #5: *Resilience, Courage, and Self-Control*

A resilient and courageous spirit is a great trait to instill in your child. These qualities will act as an umbrella during the storm of life, shielding them from any challenges they may experience. Teaching your children resilience and courage can be accomplished in a number of ways. For example, let's say they are learning to ride a bike. If they fall off, comfort them and make sure they are okay, but then help them have the courage to get back on for another ride!

Some of the challenges they face will likely correlate to their own self-control, which they can start to build from a young age. Allow them to have treats, but let them know they will only get a certain amount for a specific time period. If they eat them all and get sick, they will experience some of those natural consequences we mentioned in a previous chapter. Not only will they be ill, but they will also be out of treats and learn to have more self-control in the future.

Helping Your Toddler Develop Specific Traits

During the grand adventure of parenting, you'll get countless moments that allow you to shape your child's character. While this process isn't an exact science, there are a few ways you can facilitate the development of certain qualities. Though seemingly innate, traits like empathy and kindness need careful cultivation and reinforcement. It may be easier to think of these traits like seeds and you the gardener. Even though it may take years for these traits to bloom fully, it's important to plant the seeds in early life and tend to their growth carefully.

Tips to Teach Empathy and Kindness

- **Model Good Behavior and Create an Empathetic Environment:** The best way for your toddler to learn any behavior is to create an environment that exemplifies the specific traits or qualities of that behavior. Take every opportunity to model empathy and kindness while with your child and make sure that they see examples of good behavior frequently. This can mean nursing a wounded bird back to health, carrying groceries for an elderly neighbor, or making a hearty chicken soup for a loved one sick with the flu. By living the values we want our children to learn, we make their world a rich garden filled with kindness and empathy.

- **Praise and Reinforce:** Seeds need regular watering, and positive reinforcement can act as a nourishing rain to foster growth. Give them credit for their good deeds, and you'll be surprised at how quickly their empathy grows. By using positive language, you can help your toddler associate good behavior with good feelings. In addition to praise, you can also give them positive titles like "little helper"; this will encourage them to embody the identity of a helper in their everyday lives.

- **Help Your Child Understand Their Own Feelings:** Empathy is all about putting yourself in someone else's shoes and understanding their perspective, and that starts with understanding our own. Ask your child how they are feeling, encourage them to explore their own emotions, and teach them to label their feelings as a way to understand their depth. You can make this process more effective by watching videos or reading books with your toddler about the experiences of others. While almost any book or movie will do, try to choose ones that involve children going through the same situations your child has gone through. This will help them draw parallels between their perspective and the perspective of the characters, which can lead them to resonate with emotions beyond their own.

- **Provide Opportunities to Be Kind:** Provide your toddler with ample opportunities to practice the art of being kind. By letting them help out or perform small acts of kindness, you can allow them to feel the positive emotions associated with being friendly and charitable. You can also play roleplaying games to teach your toddler about different feelings or ways to be kind. Even if no people are around to help, your child can learn by practicing kindness with their stuffed animals. It doesn't take much: just bringing their stuffed animals a fake cup of tea or moving them into a comfortable chair (followed by praise) can get them in the right mindset.

Tips to Teach Respect

- **Define Respect:** When you first introduce the concept of respect to your child, they may have difficulty grasping what you mean. The best way to get the point across is to give the idea of respect a clear definition. You can craft your description in any way you like, but the conversation can go something like this. "Sweetie, respect is about thinking and acting in a way that shows you care about someone else's boundaries and well-being." To simplify it, you could say it's about "talking nice and acting nice."

- **Show Them Respect's Rewarding Fruits:** It's imperative to help your child realize the positive impact of respectful behavior. One way to do this is to do what I call "Respect Storytime." This involves telling them triumphant stories (fictional or otherwise) about respectful girls and boys. You can use these stories to show your children the benefits of being respectful. These stories can have any number of themes but try to focus on illustrating how respect can open doors, make friendships blossom, and promote a fulfilling sense of self-worth.

- **Help Them Practice Patience:** A big part of being respectful involves being patient. One way to teach your toddler patience is to show them how to take turns. At their next play date, give your child a toy that you know other kids will want to play with too. Encourage your child to share the toy and wait patiently for their turn to play again, praising them when they do so.

- **Make the Process Fun:** Just like with empathy roleplay, we can play games to help teach our children respect. Simon Says is a good one to use, but it's best to play a specific version I call Simon Says Please. In this version, you can instruct your child to say "please" before they say an action. In addition to Simon Says Please, you can do a pictorial quiz. This involves showing your child pictures of respectful and disrespectful acts, after which you ask them to point to the one they believe is respectful. These interactive games can make your lessons stick in your children's minds, so eventually, respect will come naturally to them.

Tips to Encourage Learning and Exploration

- **Help Them Discover Passions and Interests:** One of the greatest gifts you can give your children is the freedom to discover what excites them. It's essential to feed the fire of their passion and encourage any interests you see bubbling up. We made it a point to expose our children to various experiences: from vibrant tunes at a local concert (with earplugs, of course) to exotic animals at the zoo, you'll be able to see what activities pique your little one's interest.

- **Give Them Hands-On Experiences:** With their innate curiosity, Toddlers are very much like little explorers, and nothing quite quenches their curiosity like hands-on experiences. They usually have an easier time understanding a concept if they can reach out and grab it. You can see this in the toys we give them, like building or sorting blocks; these toys not only hold our toddler's short attention but also offer educational value.

- **Find Their Learning Style and Make it Fun:** There are several different learning styles, including auditory (hearing), kinesthetic (touching), and visual (seeing). Our daughter, for example, was a visual learner; she would soak in every image and scene she saw like a little sponge. Find what your child responds to most frequently and introduce that style into fun and exciting lessons.

- **Provide Ample Support:** Like every explorer, your intrepid toddler may encounter hurdles, face discouragement, or grapple with insecurities. As a parent, you'll act as a lighthouse: your beacon of light will shine through the fog, offering them guidance and support. Your child may get discouraged during many learning or exploration experiences, and that's okay. Talk to them about any anxiety they are having, and try to redirect their attention in a way that helps without harming the learning process.

With These Traits, Your Toddler is Set to Be a Social Butterfly

Empathy, respect, and a passion for learning are qualities that can make every part of life better. These traits can come in handy when we consider something like socialization, which is vital to your toddler's development. In our next chapter, we'll examine why socialization is important, how to develop your toddlers' social skills, and ways to find playmates for your child to have fun with.

Dad Hacks from Chapter 7

Trait Development Hack #1: Be an Example For Your Toddler. You are the best teacher your child will ever have, and your behavior serves as a framework for how they will act. Try to be empathetic, respectful, and passionate in as many parts of your life, and your toddler will do the same.

Trait Development #2: Praise Efforts, Not Just Achievements. While crossing the finish line is always exciting, the journey to get there is just as important. Don't only encourage your child when they are succeeding, praise them when they are trying as well.

Trait Development #3: Look For Everyday Learning Opportunities. Every day is filled with tiny opportunities to teach your children valuable life lessons. If you buy some veggies from the store, tell your child briefly about the way they are grown. If you see someone struggling with a door, show your toddler how to help them open it. These small lessons build up and can make your child more excited to learn and exhibit good behavior.

Trait Development #4: Use a "Value Box." Take a box or jar and fill it with important values written on slips of paper. Each week, have your toddler draw a paper from the value box. Throughout the week, discuss that value and try to practice it in ways your toddler can understand. This can be a fun and engaging way for them to understand the concept behind certain qualities.

Trait Development #5: Engage in Random Acts of Kindness. Never pass up an opportunity to help others, especially when your child is around. This can be anything from helping someone find their lost pet to volunteering at a local shelter. Bring your toddler along and explain to them what you're doing and why it's important. This can inspire them to do the same later in life.

Chapter 8

Meeting Near the Tiny Water Cooler: Why Socializing Your Toddler is Essential

As parents, we design almost all of the social interactions our toddlers encounter. I mean, it's not as if your toddler is heading out for drinks after work, meeting the boys down at the courts for some pickup basketball, or headed to a convention to talk about insurance policies. Despite their inability to schedule their own meetings, many toddlers crave social experiences. Not only that, but socialization plays a crucial role in shaping their development. While some toddlers are naturally social, others may need a gentle nudge to get going in the right direction. I'll give you an example.

While my daughter is incredibly creative and intelligent, she does tend to be a bit more reserved. My son, on the other hand, is a social butterfly, quick to jump into the fray and start up a conversation with anyone. When we would head to the playground, my daughter would often hang back and watch as my son raced to the jungle gym to talk with the other kids. Remembering my own youthful tendency towards shyness, I decided to talk to her.

"Hey honey, I just want to let you know that it's okay to be nervous about making new friends," I said as we sat near the edge of the playground. "If you want, I can go over with you and we can say hello together." She smiled, squeezed my hand, and together we introduced ourselves to the jungle gym crew. After a few minutes I began to talk to other parents nearby, and before I knew it, my daughter was running around with her new friends, sharing toys, and playing make-believe.

While it may seem better to let children do their own thing, you don't want them to fall into the habit of being isolated. Let's look at a few of the reasons why social interaction is essential for toddlers.

6 Reasons That Show Why Socialization is Important for Toddlers

Reason #1: *Boosts Their Chatterbox Skills*

Ever notice how your toddler always seems to be babbling away? Well it isn't all babble; what you are actually seeing is the brain's language centers developing and adapting to the world around them. Social interactions, whether they be with adults or your toddler's pint-sized peers, can supercharge this development process. The more conversations your child has, the richer their vocabulary and comprehension will become.

Reason #2: *Unleashes Their Inner Creativity*

Your child is probably playing make-believe all on their own, but you know what can power their imagination even more? Socialization! An environment that provides ample social interactions will help your toddler explore their abstract thinking abilities. Conversations often require creativity to navigate, and your child will get many chances to innovate during social interactions.

Over time, their improvisational skills will grow and blossom, allowing them to discuss a variety of topics.

Reason #3: *Ignites Their Confidence*

The more your toddler socializes, the more they will gain the confidence to communicate clearly. This process usually starts by learning to communicate their needs; over time, they'll begin to build a strong sense of self. As they discover who they are, they'll be much more willing to interact and learn from the world around them. This confidence can form the foundation for the way they're perceived, both in their childhood and in the academic or career paths they walk as an adult.

Reason #4: *Trains Them for Teamwork*

Teamwork makes the dream work, and your toddler will need to learn how to play nice if they want to get ahead in life. The roots of cooperation grow from the rich soil of social interaction, and your child will learn how to work together as they grow with their group of friends or classmates. This cooperation can take almost any form, including working together to build a sandcastle or teaming up for a group game of pretend. As they age, teamwork skills will help them do group projects at school, participate in team sports, and eventually work with their colleagues during their careers.

Reason #5: *Nurtures Their Social Butterfly Wings*

Your child has learned to walk; now it's time to fly. Building the skills it takes to be a social butterfly is all about trial, error, and practice. Each interaction, whether it be tussling over a toy or giggling over a goofy face, is a chance to learn about the best ways to share, cooperate, and show respect. Before you know it, your child will be able to flutter around confidently in any social setting, making them well-prepared for future interactions and relationships.

Reason #6: *Builds Up Their Empathic Abilities*

Being able to put yourself in another person's shoes and see things from their perspective are essential skills, both of which can be built up during social outings. As your child talks to others, they will slowly learn how they think and feel. This, in turn, nurtures their ability to empathize. Using their newfound understanding, your toddler will be able to better respond to different situations and emotions. This will carry on into adulthood, allowing them to navigate complex social situations with grace and understanding.

How to Develop Your Toddler's Social Skills

So now that we know why social skills are important, how do we help our children develop them? While the task may seem daunting, there are endless ways you can introduce socialization into your toddler's life. Here are a few ways that I've found to be particularly effective.

- **Tiny Networking Events:** While your toddler might not be ready to create a Facebook profile and send invites to classmates or coworkers, they do love the stimulating atmosphere of a group playdate. Because their networking skills are limited, setting up these playdates will be up to you. If you have friends that are parents as well, this can be easy; if not, you may have to look to local daycares or online parenting groups to set up one on your own. Whatever environment you choose, make sure it is supportive, safe, and filled with potential activities.

- **Play Pretend:** Encourage your child to engage in make-believe; while they do, try to participate in their pretend worlds and help them simulate different social situations. If they set up a tiny restaurant, order a faux burger and some fake fries; if they have a tiny plastic stethoscope on, let them check your heartbeat (just don't let them prescribe you any medication!) These situations teach them about different social roles and further allow them to empathize with the situations of others. They'll also allow them to use their problem-solving skills, which will come in handy during real social interactions later on.

- **Social Stories and Helpful Tips:** You can use storytime to further educate your children on the social encounters they may have and provide them tips for the right way to act when talking to others. This means teaching them about eye contact, how to use polite words like "thank you", "please", and "sorry", and the right times to greet someone and say goodbye.

- **Keep Expectations Realistic and Reinforcement Positive:** We all want our toddlers to blossom into little socialites as quickly as possible, but it's important to remember that change is slow. Keep your expectations realistic for your child's social development and praise their progress. It's important to celebrate each step your child reaches and let them comfortably develop at their own pace.

Activities That Can Teach Your Children Sharing, Problem-Solving, and Good Manners

In addition to the techniques above, there are a wide range of activities you can use to teach your children valuable social skills. Let's look at a couple of examples of ways to show your children the joy of sharing, how to overcome problem-solving challenges, and the best ways to display good manners when talking to others.

Activities to Show that Sharing is Caring

Activity #1: *Toy Trade Marketplace*

Ever notice how your child will get bored with a toy, then the second another kid picks it up, it's suddenly the thing they want most? These instances are a great opportunity to encourage your child to share, take turns, and compromise. Ask your child if they'd be willing to wait or trade toys with their friend instead of having a tantrum. This can be challenging at first, but eventually, they'll stop focusing on the tears and start focusing on the positive (a different toy to play with!)

Activity #2: *Board Game Battles*

While some parents may see board games as a harrowing battleground, they can also be a great way to teach your children about taking turns and delayed gratification. Pick simple games they can understand and help them with the more difficult parts of the game. If possible, pick a game that involves teamwork, as this can add further educational value to the activity.

Support Your Little Sleuth: Activities to Enhance Problem-Solving

Activity #1: *Unblock Their Potential*

Building blocks or legos are some of the best ways to make problem-solving fun for your child. Give them challenges, like "build a tower as high as you can" or "try not to eat any of the legos this time." Work together with them and talk to them while they complete their building. This activity will help them overcome obstacles, experience what it's like to discuss problems as they occur, and even laugh if they end up failing.

Activity #2: *Puzzle It Out*

Busting out a puzzle and working on it with your child is a great way to enhance their problem-solving skills. Make sure it isn't too complex; I recommend starting simple and moving up if they seem to be getting the hang of it. Talk them through any frustrations they have and gently remind them that a pity-party won't solve that puzzle. Of course, you'll also want to help them if they are struggling, as this can further their understanding of teamwork.

The Tender Toddler: Activities to Teach Good Manners

Activity #1: *Model the Magic Words*

While more of a tip and less of a one-time activity, modeling good manners is one of the fastest ways to get your children pick up on positive socialization habits. A good place to start is by using the three corners of the good manners triangle: "please", "thank you", and "I'm sorry." Show your toddler the right time to deploy these magic words, and congratulate them when they use each one appropriately.

Activity #2: *Manners at Mealtime Mean Dessert After*

Another social activity that requires good manners is meal time, and teaching your toddler the details of fine dining can ensure dinner is a bit less messy. Have them set the table, put out (non-sharp) silverware, and let them distribute napkins. Yes, this will sometimes mean that forks will fall to the floor before they make it to the table, but it's all about baby steps. If they complete their dinner tasks successfully, surprise them with a bit of dessert. This will help reinforce those good manners in their mind for next time!

Finding Playmates and Planning Playdates

If you don't already have friends, neighbors, or relatives with children, finding playmates for your children may take some time. Fortunately, there are a few ways you can kick-start this process. Start by looking for parenting or playgroups on social media. Facebook will usually have some groups in your area, though it's always important to check them out in person before bringing your child. If you can't find any, you could consider starting your own. You can also find playmates at family-friendly events. It may seem awkward, but strike up a conversation with another family while you are attending with your children. You'd be surprised how many people are eager to find playmates as well!

Another great way to find playmates is to enroll your child in daycare or preschool. Daycare is great for children that haven't quite reached preschool age; they'll be closely attended to as they interact with other kids their age and have a blast playing games and eating snacks. Once your child reaches the right age, preschool is a very effective way to boost your child's development. In addition to socialization, a good preschool will help them develop their cognitive and motor skills as well.

5 Ideas for Positive Play Dates

1. **Get a Little Crafty:** Organize a crafts day and let your playgroup get hands-on with some macaroni, non-toxic glue, paints, and sparkles. Actually, leave the sparkles at home, they are a nightmare to clean up.

2. **Have Some Fun with Food:** Have a little "cooking" class with your toddler's playgroup by letting them build their own snacks. These can be as simple as crackers, cheese, and meat, but you can free-style this is any way you like.

3. **Lights, Shadows, Action:** Time to put on a show! Teach your group how to make different shadow puppets, and try your best to put on a collaborative show. It will almost certainly be a disaster, but I promise it will be tons of fun.

4. **Toddler Tango:** Turn on that dance music and get to movin'! In addition to getting your toddler comfortable with expressing themselves amongst their peers, this activity also burns off some of that boundless energy that children can have. Believe me, naptime will be soon to follow.

5. **The Great Outdoors:** It's important to get out in nature, and what better way to do so than with friends? If the parents of your group are comfortable and some agree to chaperone, plan a day trip. This can be out to a simple walking trail, or to a fun activity like mini-golf. Either way, let your kids soak up some sunshine!

Your Toddler Has a Playdate, but What Will They Wear?

As dads, it can be a bit hard to know what the current fashion trends are for toddlers (or even ourselves, really.) In our next chapter, we'll look at some ways that you can create a functional and fashionable wardrobe, how to pick out outfits for special events, and what it means to "accessorize."

Dad Hacks from Chapter 8

Socialization Hack #1: Collaboration is Crucial. When designing activities for your toddlers to engage in with others, try to include an element of teamwork. This can mean having them all paint together on the same canvas, work in tandem to create fun crafts, or assemble snacks for one another. Think of it like a team-building exercise for toddlers; they'll learn to share, collaborate, and solve problems as a group.

Socialization Hack #2: Don't Just Share Toys, Share Feelings. A big element in developing social skills is empathy, and that starts with understanding emotions. Encourage your toddler to share their feelings and tell you the emotions they are experiencing.

Socialization Hack #3: Use Stuffed Animals as Stand-ins. It's not always possible to get a playdate together, but your children can roleplay with their stuffed animals or favorite toys. Give them scenarios to play out and teach them the right way to handle different situations. This will make the real thing that much easier!

Socialization Hack #4: Baby Book Club. You probably already read on a regular basis with your kids, but it can be helpful to add in a bit of discussion afterwards. Talk about the character's feelings and actions, and ask your child what they think about them. This will further their understanding of social cues and how different contexts relate to real-life social interactions.

Socialization Hack #5: Talk, Talk, Talk. Engage your toddler in conversations as much as possible, whether it be about toys, tv shows, snacks, or anything else they are passionate about. Their vocabulary may be limited, but the more you talk, the more words they will pick up along the way.

Chapter 9

Clothing Chaos and Wardrobe Wars: Dressing Your Toddler for Success

If you're like me, you probably don't keep up to date on the latest trends emerging from the world of fashion. Most dads (myself included) are perfectly content to throw on the same pair of jeans we've been wearing for a week, cover our messy hair with a ball cap, and fish out our one good button-up shirt when we're told to "put on something nice for tonight." Unfortunately, this method of messy dressing won't cut it for your child. Not only can a good outfit boost your child's confidence and allow them to socialize more easily, it can also serve a number of other functional purposes.

For example, good clothes can help your child deal with the elements. To ensure your toddler is comfortable, happy, and safe, you'll need to match your outfits with the current season or inclement weather. Consider the best ways to shield your toddler from rain, wind, sun, or snow; in most cases, you'll need several different clothing items to deal with these conditions. The chilly months will require a well-insulated jacket or sweater, the wet months of spring are best weathered with a good rain jacket, and lightweight, breathable fabrics will help cool them off during the summer.

Another thing to consider is that the act of dressing your child won't always be easy. Even though you are only trying to help them by dressing them, you may still face resistance. I can tell you I've had some epic battles trying to get my children to get their clothes on so we can make it somewhere on time. Socks fly across the room, clothes go into ceiling fans, and if you aren't careful, you'll start your day with a naked toddler streaking out into the street.

The way to avoid these wars is to find a wardrobe your child can get excited about. A good goal to have during this journey should be to simplify the dressing process as much as possible. One of the best ways to do this is with a little fashion technique known as the "capsule wardrobe."

Simple, Functional, and Fun: How Capsule Wardrobes Can Solve Your Fashion Frustrations

So what is a capsule wardrobe? Basically, it's a set of essential clothing items that don't go out of fashion (so they are kind of in a "time capsule.") This wardrobe can include a variety of shirts, pants, coats, and anything else your child likes to wear. Capsule wardrobes simplify the process of dressing your children by creating a set of different outfits you can mix and match. You'll also save space, as more matching clothes means fewer individual outfits clogging up your child's wardrobe. Plus, because everything looks good with everything else, you can allow your child to choose their clothes without fear they will look like they got caught in a tornado in the child's section of a secondhand store.

How to Create a Capsule Wardrobe for Your Kids

1. **Find the Essentials:** A foundational quality of a good capsule wardrobe is versatility. Choose basic items that you could pair with pretty much anything. You also want to choose weather or season-appropriate clothing to swap out when necessary. This can include:

   - Solid colored t-shirts

   - Neutral-toned button-down shirts

   - Blue jeans

   - Simple skirts

   - Dark-colored underwear and socks (for stains) Heavy coats (for winter)

   - Sweaters or hoodies (for fall)

   - Raincoats

   - Light jackets

   - Matching shoes (or boots for rainy season)

   As for the quantity, I recommend having 5-8 tops, 4-6 bottoms, 1-2 sweaters or coats, 1-2 dresses or rompers, 7 pairs of underwear, 7 pairs of socks, 2 pairs of shoes, 2 pairs of pajamas, and 1-2 outfits for special occasions. Of course, the amount you go with is up to you. I also often choose clothes with snaps or zippers, as these are easier to operate than buttons. Plus, it's less likely that your children will try to tear off a zipper and eat it (the same can't be said about buttons, which toddlers seem to find quite appetizing.)

A note about seasonal items: make sure to rotate out parts of your capsule as winter or summer approaches. Because a capsule wardrobe is designed so your child could pick out their own clothes, you wouldn't want them accidentally wearing a winter coat in summer or forgetting to wear a sweater when it's cold.

2. **Let Your Child Choose:** Capsule wardrobes should be crafted to match your child's individual style while remaining simplistic enough that they can choose what outfit they would like to wear. You should also include your child in the decision-making process for some of the purchases. Let them point out a few pieces that show their personality, whether it be a t-shirt with their favorite superhero on it, a dress decorated with their favorite type of flower, or a light-up pair of sneakers that display their favorite colors. Having some personal touches in their wardrobe will make them more excited about getting dressed, and may kickstart their interest in learning to dress themselves.

3. **Quality Over Quantity:** While a traditional wardrobe may have dozens of different clothing items in it, a capsule wardrobe is all about efficiency. Because you'll want the select few pieces in the closet to last, it's essential to buy high-quality and durable fabrics. These clothes will likely be washed many times, and you want them to hold up to the frequent wear and tear they may face over their lifetime.

4. **Check-in and Adjust:** Your child's preferences will change over time, and you want them to be happy with what they are wearing. Capsule wardrobes are flexible and can be updated whenever you like, but it's good to do so on a semi-regular basis. Every few months, check in with your child and ask if there are any pieces of clothing they no longer enjoy wearing. You can swap these out for new ones or trade with another parent if your children wear similar sizes.

Dressing Your Tot For Special Occasions

Whether it's a big Christmas party, a family wedding, or a birthday for a loved one, your toddler will get more into the event if they dress up. Your child will see you donning your best suit and tie and, like so many other parts of life, will want to copy you.

It's good to have a couple of outfits you can dress your children up in for special occasions, though the task may be a bit more challenging than it sounds. To start, you'll want to make sure you get something that matches the occasion. There's no reason to get a tiny tuxedo for your child to wear to a casual family gathering; on the other end of the spectrum, a Minions costume wouldn't be appropriate for a wedding. Try to find a functional outfit for formal events (a nice mini-suit or dress) and a less formal button-down or blouse.

You'll also want to ensure that whatever you choose, it's comfortable. I can't tell you how painful it is to pick out a nice suit for your son, only to have him wrenching at the arms of his jacket and crying out in the middle of a ceremony. Make sure that the clothes aren't too tight or too loose and that the fabric comfortably interacts with your child's skin. It's important to let them try the outfit on before you buy it, and even once you do, have them wear it for a few hours before the event. The clothes should also be simple, so you aren't wrestling with complicated buttons when the "I'm about to pee my pants" shot clock is counting down. Even with this preparation, accidents still happen, so bring a spare change of clothes just in case.

Just like with your capsule wardrobe, it's also vital to keep the weather in mind. That button-down isn't going to cut it in winter, and a heavy suit jacket could leave your child sweating in the spring or summer. If the event is outdoors, you'll want to keep the sun in mind. A nice hat can keep your child from being blinded or sunburned. Of course, your child may have their preferences of what they want to wear (and you should consider their opinions.) But if they are trying to wear something too thick on a hot day, you'll have to shut it down.

Time to Accessorize

As a dad, you may not know what the word "accessorize" even means (I know I didn't.) But oddly enough, it's something you probably do with your own outfits every day. Accessorizing basically refers to the "extras" we put on in addition to the basic shirt-and-pants foundation of our outfits. So for dads, that means watches, sunglasses, hats, and belts. For your toddlers, it can mean the same items and more (except maybe a watch. I mean, it's not like they have appointments to keep.)

3 Tips to Help Your Toddler Accessorize

Tip #1: *Keep it Age-Appropriate and Comfortable*

Yes, it might seem cool to put a little cuff pin or pocket square on your child's suit; it's important to remember to keep an appropriate outfit age appropriate. It's entirely possible your child will pull off smaller items and try to swallow them, and everything they wear is at risk of being dirtied or damaged. Don't give your child any accessories that are fewer than centimeters (1 ¼ inches) in diameter or smaller than 6 centimeters (2 ¼ inches) in length; that way, they can't get lodged in their windpipe.

In addition, you'll want to make sure anything you give them is comfortable. Sure, it seems like a funny idea to give your child a top hat and monocle so they look like the Monopoly Man at your brother's wedding. But it will be less funny when their hat slips down over their eyes, they trip, and their expensive monocle smashes on the ground. Basically, anything that may hurt them or hinder their movement is an absolute no-go.

Tip #2: *Let Them Add Their Own Flair*

If you have some extra jewelry, bracelets, belts, or scarves that are event and weather-appropriate, let your toddler choose from a few to personalize their outfit. Of course, you'll want to keep this within reason. If your toddler is left to their own devices, they may layer on a ridiculous number of necklaces or bows.

In addition to avoiding over-accessorizing, you'll want to ensure that none of the items are small enough to swallow or so outrageous they'll cause a scene. I remember one of the accessories my daughter brought to a family reunion was her hamster, Charles. We didn't find that Charles was attending the event until we saw him being chased by my mother's dog, Max, through the backyard barbeque. Luckily for Charles, Max knocked over a freshly cooked plate of hamburgers during his chase and stopped to go for the easier meal.

Tip #3: *Good Shoes are a Must*

One of the most common complaints I hear from my children when we're attending a special event is, "Dad, my feet hurt!" While comfy shoes are important no matter the occasion, it can be challenging to deal with a foot emergency if you are at a wedding or party far from home. If you are attending an event that calls for formal or dress shoes, make sure to bring backups in case your children experience any discomfort. You'll also want to consider the weather. If the forecast calls for rain (even a slight chance), you'll want to back some rubber boots. If there may be snow, an extra pair of socks or warm boots can be a lifesaver.

We're Well Into Our Journey; It's Time to Take a Rest

We've covered a lot of topics so far and dealt with a number of ways to properly take care of your toddler. But what about taking care of yourself? As a dad, maintaining your own mental and physical health is essential. If you aren't operating at your best, how can you give your best to your child? In our next chapter, we'll talk about some self-care tips you can use to ensure you're ready to step up to the plate each day and continue batting a thousand.

Dad Hacks from Chapter 9

Wardrobe Hack #1: Safety First. While taking a beautiful family photo or giving your child some fashion freedom is important, the absolute #1 priority is safety. Make sure any items you choose for your child, or items they choose for themselves, are appropriate for their current development level and the environment they'll be wearing them in.

Wardrobe Hack #2: Trading Saves Money. It's fine to go on a bit of a shopping spree every now and then, and I wouldn't try to stop you from getting your child a lovely new set of clothes or some accessories they are excited about. But it's essential to keep in mind that your toddler is going to grow quickly. Many of these clothing items will be too small in a short amount of time. To avoid waste, consider trading or reusing older clothes. Trading with other parents and using hand-me-downs is a great way to remain frugal and avoid waste.

Wardrobe Hack #3: Take Capsule Pictures. Photos can make the already simplified process of using capsule wardrobes even easier. Lay out each of your outfit combinations and take a photograph, giving them labels if you need them to be more easily identifiable (i.e., Summer Time #1, Winter Time #1, etc.) Then, finding an outfit is as easy as pointing at one of the photos. This can also make it simpler for your child to dress themselves (once they get to that point in their development.)

Wardrobe Hack #4: Let Them Have a Bit of Fun. It's understandable not to allow your child to dress the exact way they want every single day. There are practical reasons for this (toddlers may not understand that clothes can get dirty or could wear a piece of clothing that may endanger them in certain weather) and personal reasons (you don't want your child to dress like a dinosaur to graduation). That being said, let them go wild every once and a while. It will encourage them to be creative, and you'll get some great photos to embarrass them with later.

Wardrobe Hack #5: Getting Out Tough Stains Can Be Simple. Your child will inevitably take the carefully planned outfit you chose and run it through all manner of mud, food, and filth. For particularly tough stains, I use a mixture of dish soap, hydrogen peroxide, and baking soda. The measurements don't have to be exact, but I recommend using a teaspoon of each and gauging whether you need to add more to the mixture. Scrub that concoction into the stain and leave it overnight. Then rinse it off and send it through the wash. This can work great for grease and other stubborn stains.

Chapter 10

Me T.I.M.E.: The Best Way For Dads to Practice Self-Care

As dads, your responsibilities often include not only your duties as a father, but your responsibilities as a partner, friend, and employee. After a while, the weight of these expectations can grow heavy and you may begin to feel a bit burned out. When this happens, some people choose to ignore the flashing check engine light shining in their brains and simply keep driving. But let me tell you a story of what happens when you ignore that warning light for a bit too long.

A while ago, I was starting to feel the telltale signs of burnout, but I thought there wasn't time to do anything about it. Instead of addressing my feelings, I decided to ignore them in order to meet my obligations at work and at home. This went on for several weeks, until one day I had to present my progress on a big project in front of several department heads. As you can imagine, my mind was a bit preoccupied before work that morning. Still, I raced around the kitchen to assemble my kids' lunches before slapping my presentation documents into my briefcase. From there I herded the children into the car and dropped them off at daycare and school. Once I got to work, I steeled myself with a piping hot cup of black coffee and entered the conference room to set up. As my coworkers took their seats, I opened my briefcase to retrieve my documents. But there weren't any documents at all. Instead, there were two peanut butter and jelly sandwiches with the crusts cut off, two small bags of sliced apples, two cookies, and two juice boxes. Unless I could somehow improvise a new presentation about the fiscal benefits of PB&J, this presentation wasn't going to go well.

While this lunch mixup may seem adorable, and my bosses were very understanding, I'm incredibly fortunate that I didn't slip-up in a more serious way. With how little sleep and self-care I was getting, I very well could have had an accident while cooking, driving, or something else dangerous. Even if I had avoided a hazardous accident, I was surely performing worse than usual at my job and as a dad. That's why taking the time to recharge and rejuvenate is so essential. The best way to start is by learning how to balance your responsibilities at work and home. Let's look at five ways you can keep dad life and work life in check.

5 Ways to Balance Work Life and Dad Life

Way #1: *Set Boundaries and Make Your Time Count*

Drawing a clear line between work and home life can be a struggle, especially if you work from home. Despite the challenge, it's important to set up some reasonable boundaries; you'll want to create a schedule that allows you to spend quality time with your family and still get your job done. Open a dialogue with your partner and try to adjust your work schedule in a way that allows you to alternate afternoons or evenings with your children. It's essential to be there for the big moments, which means prioritizing quality over quantity. It's better to have meaningful interactions where you are fully engaged rather than larger chunks of time where you can't give your children the attention they deserve.

Way #2: *Communicate and Delegate*

Solid family communication is vital. Think of it like this: instead of using a cup and some string (i.e., communicating the bare minimum), wouldn't you rather talk on a brand new smartphone? High-level communication involves speaking with your partner openly and honestly while encouraging them to do the same. Don't be afraid to discuss your work responsibilities with them, and see if it's possible to delegate some at-home tasks when your job starts to get a bit frantic. You'll also want to communicate with your supervisors or bosses, letting them know when you need things like paternity leave, family medical leave, vacation time, or a more flexible schedule. This can make a large workload much more manageable, which in turn will create a more stress-free and happy family life.

Way #3: *Bring and Build*

If you want your children to understand where you spend your time away from them, consider showing them what you do for work. Create a connection by sharing stories about your job and bring your kids to work events when it's appropriate. In doing this, you can also connect with other fathers or parents you work with and create a strong support network. You can swap stories, tips, set up playdates, and ask the other parents how they balance their home and work lives.

Way #4: *Learn to Rock and Roll with the Punches*

Being a dad is all about adapting; you'll want to stay agile and ready to jam with the ever-changing playlist of work and home. Fatherhood is a lifelong performance, and being a good role model means staying cool under pressure. There will be weeks when your boss seems to pile assignment after assignment on your desk; at other times, problems may crop up with your children or spouse. In these moments it's important to take a step back, breathe, and calmly create a plan to get through the rough patches.

Way #5: *Setting Expectations and Engaging in Self-Care*

You are only one person, and no matter who you are, there's a limit to what one dad can do. With these limitations in mind, create a realistic and reasonable set of expectations for what you can do at work and home. You may also want to talk with your spouse about areas you may need help in. Identifying these problem areas can help you find ways to get some downtime and take care of yourself. What your self-care will include can vary, but usually this means eating healthy, exercising, getting enough sleep, and spending time with your friends. These, and other activities we consider "self-care," are essential if you want to stay up on your feet and on top of your obligations.

Why is Self-Care Important for Dads?

Everyone needs time to take care of themselves, regardless of whether they are a dad or not. That being said, being a dad is a lot like being an outlet extender with too many things plugged into it. With so many responsibilities draining our power, how can we possibly get our energy back? The answer is self-care! With self-care, you can top those batteries off while improving your physical and mental health in the long term. While your kids should be your #1 priority, that doesn't mean you should neglect yourself. Focusing on your own well-being can help you manage stress, stave off potential burnout, and ensure you approach parenting with the positive energy it requires.

Not only will a solid self-care routine dramatically improve your own life, but it can also positively impact your relationships. If your mental and emotional health is in tip-top shape, you'll be able to have healthier and happier interactions with your partner and children. Plus, when your kids see you taking care of yourself with a smile, they'll learn just how important it is to maintain their own health and happiness.

Even without the health benefits, dads need to maintain a sense of identity and self outside of being a father. Don't get me wrong, your role as a dad is important, but putting energy into your hobbies, personal interests, and friendships can lead to a more fulfilling and well-rounded life. Self-care can also provide higher self-esteem and self-confidence, both of which will improve your time at home, at work, and everywhere else in your life.

So what is the best way to engage in self-care? Well, the way you recharge is entirely up to you, but there are some proven techniques you can use to get the most out of your me-time. I personally use something called "the T.I.M.E. method". Let's break down the four components of this method and see how you can apply it to your own life.

The T.I.M.E. Method for Self-Care

The T.I.M.E. method (which stands for Time, Intent, Mindfulness, and Exercise) is a structuring technique that can allow anyone to utilize their self-care time as efficiently as possible. The first step involves looking at how we can maximize our free time and why we may have more hours in the week than we think.

T: *Time*

Sometimes being a dad can feel like a plate-spinner in the circus. You're up on that stage, balancing and spinning all of these different plates, and you're trying your best not to let any of them fall. This is hard enough, so it may seem ridiculous to try to get a "me-time" plate spinning as well. Carving out a few hours amidst the demanding responsibilities of fatherhood and work can be tricky, but it isn't impossible. The key is to remember that self-care isn't an indulgence; it's an investment. The benefits of self-care far outweigh the negatives, and the boost you'll get can make other tasks in your life that much easier.

Because there are only so many hours in the day, you'll need to get creative with the ways you carve yourself out a slice of self-care pie. Remember that your "me-time" doesn't have to be taken all at once. Take advantage of those little breaks you get throughout the day: your lunch break, downtime in the evenings, or when your child is taking a nap. Use these windows of time to meditate, read a few chapters of a book, or just sit in silence and take some deep breaths.

In some cases, getting even these small moments will require establishing some new boundaries. The stronger these boundaries are, the longer chunks of time you'll get. You can start by having that discussion with your boss I mentioned before (the one regarding working outside the office.) Try to reach a compromise between total accessibility (answering emails at all times, doing work projects at home) and total freedom (deleting your boss from your contacts the moment Friday hits). In addition to getting your work in order, you can adjust your sleep schedule to wake up a bit earlier, giving yourself time alone before everyone else is awake. However, if you fit it in, try to establish significant swathes of time just for you. If all else fails, call in reinforcements. Talk to family, friends, and loved ones about times they can babysit or assist you with some household tasks. There's no shame in getting a little help!

I: *Intent*

This next section requires a bit of self-reflection. What areas of your self-care do you believe need the most attention? Is it your physical health, mental health, personal interests, or something related to your work? What are your values and goals? Answering these questions will help you define your intention and better utilize your spare time.

The majority of your intentions should be informed by the expectations you set for yourself. It's essential to be realistic and remember that life can be unpredictable. One day can go smoothly, allowing you to hit all of your scheduled events, while the next may involve a whirlwind of emergency work emails and toddler tantrums. If you don't end up getting everything done on your to-do list, that's okay. Celebrate your wins, learn from your losses, and keep in mind that any amount of self-care is a victory.

M: *Mindfulness*

If possible, try to introduce an element of mindfulness into your self-care routine. The way I do this is by starting my day with some meditation and deep breathing. Giving my brain a break from other people (and the distractions of my phone or computer) allows me to ground myself and begin my day with a clear head.

The great thing about mindfulness is that you don't need to meditate to practice it. Try focusing on your next walk, meal, or time alone; I mean really experience the moment. So often in life, we just go through the motions, slapping that auto-pilot button and letting one day blur into the next. Connect with yourself and the environment around you; you'll be shocked at how quickly your stress levels drop.

E: *Exercise*

While a self-care routine can include anything that revitalizes your spirit or recharges your batteries, I always recommend throwing some physical activity into the mix. We talked before about how beneficial exercise is for your child, but it also has a vast array of benefits for adults, including:

- Improving your cardiovascular health

- Increasing sleep quality

- Lowering the risk of chronic disease

- Boosting your mood through endorphin production

- Improving brain function

- Reducing stress and anxiety

- Improving self-confidence and self-esteem

- Increasing blood flow and oxygen to the brain

- Helping you maintain a healthy weight

- Improving your sex life

Exercise can also reduce that ever-present dad fatigue we all go through. Personally, I'd go crazy without the gym. Before I started working out, I definitely had a lower quality of life, relying on caffeine alone to give me enough energy to get through the day. Not only was I irritable and tired, but my performance at work was beginning to slip. Of course, your exercise doesn't have to involve weightlifting. Walking, running, and even using newer tech like virtual reality can help you work up a sweat and get many of the benefits listed above.

Our Journey is Almost Complete

As our time together on this toddler tip trip comes to a close, I want to talk a bit about the best ways to work with your spouse or partner as parents. In our final chapter, we'll look at the importance of working together, fruitful techniques you can use to establish parenting goals, the best ways to handle disagreements, and the best ways to support your partner or co-parent.

Dad Hacks from Chapter 10

Self-Care Hack #1: Magic Meal Prep. If you want to save time and energy that could be better spent on self-care, consider the magic of meal prepping. Find a chunk of time one day a week to cook and pack up healthy meals. It's incredible how much time this saves; plus, it lowers the chance you'll go through a drive-thru or pick up something fried or frozen on a busy day.

Self-Care Hack #2: The Mighty Power Nap. Your baby isn't the only one who can benefit from a good nap. If you find yourself with 30 minutes on your hands, draw the shades and hit the hay. Even a short rest can help give you the boost you need to push on until you can get some me-time.

Self-Care Hack #3: It Takes a Village. Support networks are a crucial element of parenting, especially if you want to find time for self-care. The materials you build your network with are up to you. Whether it's family, friends, or people you meet in parenting communities and groups, your support network can provide tips and assistance during the more difficult stretches of your parenting journey.

Self-Care Hack #4: Meditation in Your Pocket. There are a number of free meditation apps you can use to squeeze in a quick mindfulness exercise during the day. Find one you like and try to use spare moments (like while you are on break at work, waiting for a coffee, or during your baby's nap time) to find a bit of inner peace.

Self-Care Hack #5: Dad & Baby Workout Time. If you find yourself in charge of your toddler but desperately need a workout, try including your child. Going for a walk, dancing in the living room, or running around the backyard are all great ways to get both of you the physical activity you need.

Chapter 11

Every Pilot Needs a Co-Pilot: How to Parent with a Partner

The journey of parenting is a lot like piloting an international flight (yes, we are doing another analogy folks. Strap in!) You are in the cockpit, the dashboard is full of blinking lights and switches, and most of the time, you aren't quite sure which ones to press. You are responsible for precious cargo and will almost certainly encounter turbulence along the way. Sure, you may have your flight plan (or, in our case, your parenting strategy and goals), but that doesn't mean there won't be bumps during your travels. But overcoming those obstacles can be much easier if you are fortunate enough to have a spouse or co-parent. Having someone on your side can be a lifesaver when you encounter the perils of parenting, and through the power of teamwork, strong communication, and mutual support, you will almost certainly get to your destination.

It's natural for most co-parents to start off as inexperienced pilots. In our case, we weren't quite sure where we were headed, our communication channels were fraught with static, and the cockpit was often filled with sharp tones of disagreement. Though far from abnormal, the turbulence we encountered still tested our ability to work together. After a few failed potty-training sessions or sleepless nights, it's easy to forget just how vital that other person is to you. I remember one tough stretch in particular where our communication took a nosedive.

The story starts after a recent change in daycares. The new location checked all our boxes: highly rated, in a better area, and with more emphasis on outdoor activities (which my son loved.) At the time, my wife and I had been dealing with a somewhat rebellious streak from our daughter; as a result, we had been having a few more disagreements than usual. We were communicating less and less, which only served to ignite a never-ending loop of unresolved arguments. In addition to all this, I was up for a promotion at work, so most days, my mind was preoccupied with making a good impression at the office. All the ingredients were laid out for a classic mistake cake to be made, and unfortunately, my wife was the one who would bake it.

On the first day my son was meant to go to the new daycare, I received a frantic call from my wife. "He's not there!" my wife cried. "The daycare said no one dropped him off. Where is he?" An icy fear rushed into my veins, and I thought for a moment I would experience every parent's worst nightmare. My wife was upset and emotional, and we began to argue on the phone. I told her I had dropped him off, but she wasn't hearing it. Then a lightbulb went off in my head.

"Honey, which daycare are you at?"

The phone went silent for a moment, and my wife sighed heavily. She had gone to the old daycare. She apologized, picked up our son, and came in the door with her head hung low. I won't deny I felt frustrated, and part of me wanted to start another argument then and there. But instead, I started laughing, and she joined me. We held each other and decided we would call up my parents to take the kids

118

off our hands that night. We went out for dinner and took some time to reconnect. While the day was stressful, it served as a wake-up call. While we still have the occasional disagreement, we have yet to have a streak of lousy communication go on as long as that one did.

The Importance of Sticking Together and Presenting a United Front

Sometimes, parenting can feel like a classic Old West showdown: you and your toddler facing off outside a saloon at sunset. They want to stay up late, you want them to go to bed. You do your best Clint Eastwood impression, trying to hold your ground, but you seem to be losing the duel. In these moments, you need to remember you aren't a lone gunslinger. In many cases, you'll have a spouse, partner, family member, or someone else you trust there to help you face parenting challenges.

But just having support isn't enough; you'll want to ensure you are on the same team when an issue arises. Presenting a united front means working together to face the challenges of parenting. Let me give you an example: You lay down the law with your toddler, saying they can't have more sweets before dinner. Your toddler will stare up at you with teary eyes, reaching out for the locked cabinet that holds the cookies or candies, but you won't budge. Mission accomplished, right? Well, unbeknownst to you, your child scampers off to your partner, manipulating them with those same dough eyes and securing their forbidden snack.

This example illustrates one of the most important elements of presenting a united front: communication. You and your co-parent should discuss in advance what strategies you will use to handle different parenting challenges. A well-formed plan will allow you to stay consistent, and consistency makes following rules far more feasible for your child. As a result, you'll have more favorable discipline and development-related outcomes (in addition to avoiding unnecessary conflict.) But what's the best way to create these shared strategies and goals?

Creating a Battle Plan: How to Craft Shared Goals With Your Co-Parent

You and your co-parent are part of a team, and every successful team needs a game plan. A solid set of shared goals can transform parenting from a frustrating chore into a rewarding adventure. It's important to ensure that these goals support your child's development; you'll also want to make sure the expectations you set remain realistic and achievable. The best way to begin setting these goals and expectations is by sitting down with your co-parent for a strategy meeting.

If possible, try to have this meeting somewhere you can speak without interruption or distraction. Clearly communicate your goals and expectations in a way that your partner can understand and avoid any type of accusatory statements. "You need to stop getting mad when our son makes a mess" won't cut it, whereas "I think we should both try to speak calmly and thoughtfully when our son makes a mistake" is far better.

You also want to avoid fixating on the big picture during your strategy meeting. We all want to think about the future and our children's potential to grow into wonderful and successful adults, but discussing events that are too far ahead may hinder you. Instead, think about concrete, realistic short-term goals. Create a timeline for different objectives you'd like to achieve, but remain flexible; remember, development occurs at different rates for different children. For example, say you and your co-parent want your child to learn a certain amount of words within a year. If that goal isn't reached, that doesn't mean there needs to be a fight or that anything went wrong. Instead, you'll want to celebrate the progress that was made toward the goal. The objectives you set should symbolize the unity you have as parents and inform the direction you'll take when teaching your child.

Once you have your strategy, try to commit it to paper or a digital format so it can be referred to later. A physical record will also be handy for making adjustments later or updating progress on certain milestones. Keep in mind it may take a while to reach these milestones, and there is no such thing as perfect parents. You and your co-parent will have good days and bad days, but it's important not to dwell on the missteps. Instead, share a laugh, discuss what went wrong, learn from it, and move forward together as a unit.

Of course, disagreements will happen. They are a natural part of almost every relationship, not to mention a frequent occurrence during the process of parenting. Fortunately, there are good ways to handle these moments of conflict.

5 Tips to Help You Deal with Parenting Disagreements

It's an unfortunate fact, but even during the best of times, parental disagreements can crop up. These can be as silly as "Hey, did you tell our daughter that candy will make her legs stop growing? What is wrong with you?" to something far more serious and significant. No matter what the cause, you'll want to approach conflicts with a combination of tact and empathy, introducing moments of levity when appropriate to help reduce the tension. Here are a few tips you can use to get through rough spots with your co-parent.

Tip #1: *Breaks Can Be a Great Pressure Release Valve*

When you and your partner are in the parent pressure cooker 24/7 together, the heat can start to get to you. If you both start to snip at or take a negative tone with one another, it may be time to step back and get a bit of space. This space can be especially beneficial during a heated argument, as that's when our emotions can often get the better of us. The next time you feel like you might erupt like a volcano, take a 5-minute breather, go outside for some air, or walk around for a couple of minutes. In most cases, you'll be able to come back to the conversation with a cooler head.

Tip #2: *Listen Actively and Speak Carefully*

Let me paint a scenario: you're tired, you're hungry, and all you want to do is lay down. Meanwhile, your spouse is actively trying to discuss their frustrations, but your mind is a thousand miles away. Inactive listening can pour fuel on the fire of a disagreement; genuine and active listening, on the other hand, will convey that you care about your co-parent's opinions and feelings. If your partner seems frustrated during a discussion, make sure to respond carefully. Share your thoughts clearly and in a positive tone, and if you have a criticism, make it constructive.

Tip #3: *Keep Conversations Focused and Respectful*

As anyone in a long-term relationship can tell you, arguments can begin to lose focus and swerve outside of their original bounds. If you aren't careful, a disagreement about which high chair to purchase can suddenly reignite an argument you had years ago about something completely unrelated. The key is to keep conversations focused and remain respectful throughout. Doing so will help you find a viable solution and diffuse the argument sooner, not to mention set a good example for your children.

Tip #4: *Enlist the Help of a Third Party If Necessary and Be Willing to Compromise*

Not all disagreements can be solved in-house; sometimes, you need to enlist an outside consultant. Try to find someone impartial, like a therapist, mediator, or a person you and your co-parent are friends with. This third-party can give an objective opinion on what's happening and offer some advice on how to move forward. Of course, no matter what direction they provide, the solution will likely involve a compromise. It's essential you don't dig your heels in and try to "stick to your guns" when having a disagreement with your partner. Find a healthy middle ground involving concessions from both sides; that way, you both feel like your input was taken into account.

Tip #5: *Prioritize and Make Sure to Follow Through on Promises*

During the chaotic storm of an argument, it's easy to lose your sense of direction and priorities. When you are in the midst of these stressful situations, it's important to concentrate on the shared goals you have with your partner and keep your eyes focused on the ultimate objective: successfully raising your children. Your child's happiness and health should be the north star you use to navigate rough waters; always try to steer yourself back toward that guiding light. Getting through these turbulent seas is much easier when you follow through on the promises you make. If a disagreement is occurring because you failed to hold up your end of the bargain, gracefully accept that you made a mistake. You can learn from these failures and do better next time; for the most part, your partner will be understanding when you slip up.

Let's Take a Look Back on What We Learned

As we reach the end of our journey, I want to acknowledge just how many subjects we covered throughout this book. It may be hard to remember specific details later on, especially with the many tasks you'll be taking care of as a parent. To make locating a single technique or snippet easier, I've summarized the main points of each chapter in our conclusion.

Dad Hacks from Chapter 11

Co-Parenting Hack #1: Document Your Plan and Progress.
While a verbal plan can be helpful, writing down your strategy is a much more efficient way to maintain shared parenting goals. In addition, journaling your progress can help you understand just how far you've come on certain objectives. This is especially useful during those times when you feel down or frustrated with the parenting process.

Co-Parenting Hack #2: Revisit Goals on a Regular Basis.
Parenting is more like cooking than baking, meaning a bit of improvisation can be fine. In some cases, it isn't necessary to stick to rigid guidelines and strict measurements when raising your children. Your goals should remain fluid and amenable to change, as this can make it easier to deal with issues as they crop up. Revisit your goals with your partner and make adjustments as needed. This can increase the effectiveness of your strategy and help you move past roadblocks with grace.

Co-Parenting Hack #3: Be Empathetic Towards Your Co-Parent. It can be difficult to remember during a disagreement, but your co-parent may be dealing with struggles outside of your current argument. It's important to stay empathetic and consider all aspects of a person's life before throwing out accusations or angry statements. Remember, you're both in this together!

Co-Parenting Hack #4: Celebrate Wins, Big and Small.
Parenting is no cakewalk, and reaching a goal should be a cause for celebration. Take time every once and a while to have a special night together, acknowledging the hard work both of you put in and complementing each other's parenting victories. This helps

maintain morale and can give you the motivation you'll need to get through the next stumbling block or failure.

Co-Parenting Hack #5: Create a Shared Calendar. Remembering dates and times can be hard, especially when you and your co-parent both have your own calendar. Instead of struggling separately, combine your calendars into a shared digital space. This can allow you to update your calendar as soon as a new commitment or responsibility crops up, which makes it much easier to meet your obligations.

Conclusion

While the road through toddlerhood is bumpy, the satisfaction of completing this milestone is indescribable. Sure, it's one of the most arduous periods of parenthood, but it also comes with a significant set of rewards. That being said, it will almost certainly be accompanied by failures. But that's okay! Each mistake is an opportunity to learn, and you'd be hard-pressed to find a dad who hasn't slipped up along the way. The best things in life take work, and if you're anything like me, your children are undoubtedly the best things in your life.

In order to better absorb the information in this book, I think it's best to do a bit of review. Let's go chapter by chapter and highlight the main topics that were covered throughout our journey.

Chapter 1: Diving Into the Gene Pool: Nature vs. Nurture, Personality, and Developmental Milestones

Chapter 1 focused on the way genetics can influence our children's Predispositions and traits, as well as what effect the right environment can have on their development. Key points include:

- **The Role That Genes Play:** Genetic factors can determine your baby's cognitive development, how they interact with others, how they respond to their environment, and their level of curiosity.

- **Types of Temperament and Personality Traits:** Your toddler's temperament and personality will influence their activity level, biological rhythms, how approachable they are, their mood, how sensitive they are, and how well they adapt to certain situations.

- **Crafting an Environment That Fits Your Toddler:** By creating zones, establishing routines, encouraging independence, and setting up playdates, you can create an environment that maximizes your toddler's ability to reach new developmental milestones.

The chapter concluded by discussing some of these milestones, primarily those related to physical ability, language, cognition, and social/emotional health.

Chapter 2: The 3 P's of Potty Training: How To Know When Your Toddler's Toilet Time Has Arrived

Chapter 2 was all about potty training, starting with the signs to look for in order to see whether your toddler is ready to get started.

- Sign #1: They start barging in while you are in the bathroom

- Sign #2: They begin to outgrow diapers

- Sign #3: They communicate more about bathroom time

- Sign #4: They have reached the proper physical development milestones

From there, the chapter covers the 3 P's of potty training: Preparation, Practice, and Positive reinforcement. Chapter 3 closes by dispelling a few common myths surrounding toilet training and talks about what not to do during the process.

Chapter 3: Picky Eaters Anonymous: How to Survive Your Toddler's Selective Tastes

In chapter 3 we dove into the world of picky eating, specifically the genetic, developmental, and environmental factors that cause this culinary phenomenon. After that, we discussed some tips to help encourage your child to eat, and I shared one of my favorite quick treat recipes: customizable ants on a log. The chapter closes on a few "don'ts" of picky eating, including:

- Don't force feed

- Don't use food as a punishment

- Don't compare your child's eating habits to others

Chapter 4: Slumber Struggles: Strategies You Can Use to Solve Sleep-related Issues

Chapter 4 was all about sleep issues, starting with the reasons that sleep is so essential for a healthy toddler. From there, we talked about 3 signs that your toddler may not be getting enough sleep, including:

- Struggling to wake up and getting drowsy during the day

- Seeming moodier and unable to focus

- Changes in appetite, digestion, or immune system response

After that the chapter goes into how much sleep a toddler needs during different age ranges, how to transition your toddler from a crib to a bed, and what to do in order to help your child fall asleep.

Chapter 3 closes by discussing what to do if your child repeatedly leaves their bed at night and covers the best ways to deal with nightmares and night terrors.

Chapter 5: Find Shelter! The Terrible Two Tornado is Here

Chapter 5 delves into the dreaded realm of the Terrible Twos. We started by talking about what the Terrible Twos is, and the three signs that you've entered this time:

1. You notice more backtalk

2. Your toddler is becoming more curious, independent, and accident prone

3. Your toddler begins to test boundaries

The chapter goes on to discuss how to handle tantrums, and a few tips for dads to survive this time period. These tips include maintaining a sense of humor, using exercise to your advantage, and making sure to take some time for yourself.

Chapter 6: Dealing with Discipline: Techniques to Teach Your Toddler Consequences with Compassion

In our next chapter, we covered something most dads dislike: discipline. The chapter discusses how discipline can help your toddler and provides 3 tips you can use to keep discipline positive and compassionate. After that, we talked about what to avoid when disciplining your toddler, including shame, humiliation, physical punishment, isolation, neglect, unreasonable expectations, and shifting consequences. The chapter closes by covering a few ways to set age-appropriate expectations and create reasonable consequences for different toddler age groups.

Chapter 7: Cultivating Character and Building Better Humans

Chapter 7 moved into the topic of positive attributes, including five characteristics that can set your child up for success. These characteristics include:

1. A Curious and Creative Mind

2. A Kind and Empathetic Heart

3. A Sense of Fairness and Integrity

4. Responsibility and Self-Confidence

5. Resilience, Courage, and Self-Control

It then went into some tips on how to teach your child specific character traits, including those that relate to empathy, kindness, respect, learning, and exploration.

Chapter 8: Meeting Near the Tiny Water Cooler: Why Socializing Your Toddler Is Essential

In chapter 8, we discussed socialization, beginning with a few reasons why it's vital for your toddler. The chapter also covered the best ways to develop your toddler's social skills, including by setting up playdates, playing pretend, telling relatable stories, keeping expectations realistic, and giving positive reinforcement. After that, chapter 8 covers some activities that can teach your children sharing, problem-solving, and good manners, before closing on five ideas for positive play dates.

Chapter 9: Clothing Chaos and Wardrobe Wars: Dressing Your Toddler for Success

Chapter 9 was all about tiny fashion, mainly how capsule wardrobes can help remove some of the frustration of dressing your toddlers. These wardrobes are essentially an interchangeable set of shirts, pants, coats, and other items to simplify the dressing process. We discussed some ways for you to create a capsule wardrobe for your kids, what to do for special occasions, and some tips to help them accessorize.

Chapter 10: Me T.I.M.E.: The Best Way For Dads to Practice Self-Care

As a brief break from the toddler-focused topics, chapter 10 was all about self-care. The chapter opens with five ways to balance work and dad life before discussing why self-care is essential for fathers. After that, we covered the T.I.M.E. method for self-care, which is broken down into four parts:

- Time

- Intent

- Mindfulness

- Exercise

Each section illustrates a component of proper self-care and gives actionable ways to implement the elements into your current routine.

Chapter 11: Every Pilot Needs a Co-Pilot: How to Parent with a Partner

Our final chapter was all about co-parenting and how important it is to stay on the same page with your partner. The chapter starts by talking about presenting a united front to tackle issues as a team. After that, we discussed sitting down and creating a parenting strategy as a way to remain focused throughout your journey. The chapter then covers five ways to deal with parenting disagreements, including:

- Take breaks from arguments

- Listen actively and speak carefully

- Keep conversations focused and respectful

- Get the help of a third party if necessary

- Prioritize and make sure to follow through on promises

What I Want You to Take Away

I may complain from time to time about the turbulence we dads experience, but let me be clear: fatherhood has been the most rewarding part of my life. I love my children, and helping them grow is easily my crowning achievement. Yes, there are ups and downs, and the toddler years can be an especially rocky road. But I made it through, and I promise you will too.

If you enjoyed this book, I would be eternally grateful if you left a review on Amazon. Being a dad isn't easy, and if the tips in this book can make someone's life more manageable, I want to reach as many people as possible. During those tough nights, early mornings, and midafternoon tantrums, I know that the knowledge I've stored here can offer a bit of relief to stressed-out and frustrated dads.

I'll leave you on this: don't fast-forward through this part of your child's life. Soak up every sticky, screaming, stressful second. Truly experiencing the struggles of fatherhood makes those triumphs all the sweeter. And one day, I promise, you'll miss even the lowest moments of your time with your children. It's a cliche, but kids grow up so very fast. Don't blink, because you may miss it.

I wish you the best of luck in your parenting journey, and remember to believe in yourself. You've got this!

Reviews

As an independent author with a small marketing budget, reviews are my livelihood on this platform. If you enjoyed this book, I'd really appreciate it if you left your honest feedback. I love hearing from my readers, and I personally read every single review.

Join the Dads Club Community

DAD's Club: Support Group For Dads | Facebook

References

Made in the USA
Columbia, SC
24 October 2023

24907055R00083